F*CK'
BISCUITS

The Story of a Mother's Love

Jane Timms

Aaron Timms was twenty-one years old when he was paralysed in a car crash that killed his girlfriend and his best friend. Told he would never walk again, Aaron went on to prove the medical professionals wrong and within five months he walked unaided out of the spinal unit that was to rehabilitate him for life in a wheelchair.

This is his mother's story.

Copyright © 2023 Jane Timms

All rights reserved.

No part of this publication may be reproduced, distributed, or transmitted in any form or by any means, including photocopying, recording, or other electronic or mechanical methods, without the prior written permission of the publisher, except in the case of brief quotations embodied in critical reviews and certain other non-commercial uses permitted by copyright law.

The stories in this book reflect the author's recollection of events. Some names have been changed to protect the privacy of those depicted. Dialogue has been re-created from memory.

DEDICATION

To my son, Aaron. Thank you for all that you do for me and all that you are. For your fortitude, courage, wisdom and the love in your heart. Being your mother is a privilege and I am so proud of you. I will always love you with every fibre of my being. The love I have for my cub knows no bounds.

To my daughter-in-law, Amy. Thank you for being you and for the love and wisdom you continue to bring into our lives. For being an amazing mother to my granddaughter and for being the daughter I never had. I love you dearly.

To my darling granddaughter, Ava. Thank you for the joy you bring every single day. For making my life complete. I am so incredibly proud of you. You live in my heart always and I love you to the moon and back.

I could not have been the mother that Aaron needed me to be without the support and unconditional love of the network of friends and family who stood firm, held space for me and gave me strength in the times when it felt like I simply had nothing left to give. Who picked me up when I fell and gently guided me forward. I am forever grateful for the part you played, and continue to play, in my life - I love and thank you all from the very core of me.

I feel incredibly blessed to have received so much help and support in writing this book, and thank my cheerleaders for their encouragement, input and passion. On so many levels this has been a team effort. A special thank you goes out to my dear friend Leah for her professional help, and for all the laughs along the way.

It is also important to acknowledge the role played by the professionals in the NHS, including the paramedics at the scene of the accident along with the surgeons, the consultants and their teams. For all those who played a part in this journey I am immensely grateful.

And finally, to my spiritual team mates... I'm sorry it took so long!

TABLE OF CONTENTS

INTRODUCTION 1

CHAPTER ONE

    The Two of Us Against the World 5

CHAPTER TWO

    The Night My Life Changed Forever 25

CHAPTER THREE

    Pioneering Surgery 41

CHAPTER FOUR

    And Still No-One Listens 65

CHAPTER FIVE

    The Place Where Miracles Happen 71

CHAPTER SIX

    The Funeral 79

CHAPTER SEVEN

    Life in the Spinal Unit 95

CHAPTER EIGHT

    F*ck The Biscuits 153

CHAPTER NINE

Giving Back 195

CHAPTER TEN

It Never Really Ends 205

CHAPTER ELEVEN

And So the Journey Began 229

CHAPTER TWELVE

And Finally 261

INTRODUCTION

This is a story of hope, tragedy, heartbreak and ultimately spiritual awareness. This is my version. It wasn't my accident, but this is my story to share - warts and all. Every narrative has many sides and perspectives - this is mine.

To all the parents, in particular the mothers, who find themselves catapulted into the world of spinal injury I feel your pain, I feel your fear, I feel your hopelessness, I feel your uncertainty, I feel your anxiety, I feel your loneliness. I don't know them, but I feel them. I've got you, I see you. Everyone and every experience is unique, but these emotions we will all doubtless share at some point.

Why particularly the mothers? Because I was that mother, I still am. When this happened to me - and yes it does happen to you too - there was no-one who truly understood. I was blessed with an incredible support network, but no-one truly got it. Only the other mothers in the same boat, but they were going through their own pain and trust me when I say you have little left to support anyone else.

So why now? I've thought about writing this book for years but never did, mainly because of my own self-doubt and fear of judgement. There have been many times I've gotten into conversation and talked about my experience, each time people have said, "You should write a book". Then in July 2022 I found myself with some amazing people in the North of Bali and the subject of Aaron's accident came up. I was completely animated talking about it and answering their questions. Same thing: "You should write a book". This time it was so very different, it landed with me and I knew the time was right. I love how life twists and turns, how we grow and respond and instinctively know when it is time to follow our path. I was in the right place at the right time with the right people.

I will, of course, share many of the things that Aaron has told me, either at the time or since, about how he felt - but this is not his story. It is the story of a mother's love. Unrelenting and unconditional.

I hope you find something in these pages that you are able to relate to, feel inspired and comforted by, and that you feel loved and understood. Most of all I want you to find hope in your despair. Consider this book a great big hug from me. It'll be okay in the end. It always is, whatever the outcome.

A Mother's love is something
that no-one can explain,
it is made of deep devotion
of sacrifice and pain...

It is endless and unselfish
and enduring come what may
for nothing can destroy it
or take that love away...

It is patient and forgiving
when all others are forsaking.
And it never fails or falters
even though the heart is breaking...

It believes beyond believing
when the world around condemns,
And it glows with all the beauty
of the rarest, brightest gems...

It is far beyond defining,
it defies all explanation.
And it still remains a secret
like the mysteries of creation...

Helen Steiner Rice

CHAPTER ONE

The Two of Us Against the World

Being Aaron's mother is a privilege and an absolute blessing, but it is utterly exhausting at times! That's always been the case, really.

His dad, Steve, and I parted company when Aaron was only three years old. I was broken-hearted, we had moved to France but things didn't work out for us there so, long story short, I came back to the UK on my own with our son. I packed Aaron's belongings into our Mazda pickup truck, there wasn't enough room for much of my stuff, and drove all the way across France to Calais to take the ferry home, wherever that was. I arrived in Dover with no idea where we were going to live. My mum was living with my sister at the time and my dad had passed away a few years earlier so going to my parents wasn't an option. I headed to a friend's house where we ended up staying for a little while.

F*ck the Biscuits

Before I left France Steve had given me some money, it was all he had and at least it was something. I went to the bank to exchange my French francs for English pounds (this was way before Euros even existed!). It was a cold, damp, miserable day. I came out of the bank with £47, I couldn't believe it, I honestly thought I had more than that. I stood on the pavement outside the bank. The sky was dark, it was raining slightly and there was a cold wind blowing around us. As I stood there I looked down at the cash in my hand, then to Aaron who was perched on my hip, wondering what the hell I was going to do. We were homeless and pretty much penniless.

I smiled at Aaron. He was such a beautiful child, with stunning blue eyes and the lightest of blonde hair. When that little boy looked at me and smiled, he took all my troubles away. As long as I had him by my side I knew everything would be okay. I smiled back and said out loud, "Well, on the bright side, it can't get any worse. It's upwards from here for us". It was from this point that I built a new life for Aaron and me.

The Two of Us Against the World

After moving no less than thirteen times in the space of around ten months, having no doubt that we had regularly outstayed our welcome on friends' sofas, I was finally allocated a beautiful home in the village where I grew up. It was one of four newly-built houses owned by a housing association. I couldn't believe my luck. Before I was given the keys I drove past the house and pulled into a layby next to it so I could take a sneaky peek at our new home. The relief was palpable, it had been a long while since I felt safe but now I could give Aaron a home, somewhere to call our own for as long as we wanted. As I started to imagine decorating his room and the life we could lead there, the tears came. And boy did they come! Floods of them, I started to wonder if they would ever stop. Tears of relief, tears of pain, tears of despair, tears of happiness.

We made so many happy memories in our little home, even though things were often far from easy. At times I felt so tired of having to fight for myself, always having to face life's battles on my own, not having a partner to pick me up when I was down or to share the load. No-one to discuss things with and decisions made alone. There was usually a boyfriend lurking in the background somewhere but no-one that I would trust to help me raise Aaron. We had little in the way of disposable income and I worked hard to give Aaron the life he deserved. With no financial support I had to work long hours to cover our needs, yet still felt a deep and embedded guilt that I didn't provide enough. Regardless, there was always a decent meal on the table, fun Christmases with gifts aplenty and birthdays were the same.

Our first Christmas alone together was one of the most memorable, we had little in the way of money so we made gifts for our friends and family. We also made our own decorations. We were blessed to live in a beautiful village and one cold morning we wrapped up warm and went in search of pine cones, holly, twigs and anything else we could find. We had hours of fun wandering around the woods and fields, chatting away and sharing precious moments as we discovered all the beauty that nature has to offer, before returning home to hot chocolate and marshmallows. It was magical.

The Two of Us Against the World

We assembled our decorations and as we sat at the table, surrounded by mess and covered in glue and glitter, I glanced across at Aaron. My heart was filled with such love and pride, his enthusiasm for our little project was obvious and authentic, he was so proud of his creations. It was days like these that totally negated any struggles and made everything worthwhile.

Christmases were always special, I bought him a brand new red bike one year. I was so excited covering it in wrapping paper on Christmas Eve, hoping he'd like it as much as I thought he would. I needn't have worried, he absolutely loved it. He spent the entire day on it, riding up and down the driveway with a beaming smile on his face, it was a sheer pleasure to watch. Aaron enjoyed that bike for many years, it was worth every penny.

Every birthday party was on a budget, certainly by today's standards, but they were great. Old-fashioned games, simple food and a homemade cake. Every year without fail I made Aaron a football pitch cake, I'm not exactly a domestic goddess when it comes to such things so this cake was ideal. Simply a rectangle sponge with green royal icing on top, a football pitch drawn on with an icing pen and the same plastic nets and players came out every year. Easy, effective and big enough to feed hordes of kids, perfect. I did attempt a hedgehog cake one year but the less said about that the better!

On the day we moved into our new home I met one of my neighbours, Sue, and we quickly became the best of friends. She is still one of my closest friends today, and I know she will always be. Sue is a good, honest, kind and caring human being. I have so much respect for her, for her integrity and her courage, and her uncanny knack of always knowing the right thing to do. She gets me. I get her. My world feels safe with her in my life. She is hilariously funny too and never fails to put a smile on my face. Her daughter is slightly younger than Aaron and we brought the children up together, sharing our struggles and sometimes sharing our food!

It was tough at times but we did have a lot of laughs along the way. Sue has the ability to make me belly laugh. She always has my back, and I will always have hers. We often seem to be able to read each other's minds and this came in very useful on the day we went to see Robbie Williams live at The Bowl in Milton Keynes. We arrived, parked the car and started heading towards the stadium. As we walked around the corner, we just stood still and looked at each other. The queue was phenomenal. People must have been there all night to secure a place at the front of the line, and the end was so far away that we couldn't see it from where we stood. We were standing adjacent to the front of the queue, the entrance to the stadium, when we noticed a gap in the barrier and the security guard next to it was somewhat sidetracked by a pretty young blonde woman. We shot each other glances and without a word spoken between us, we knew the plan. As we crept through the gap and ran to the entrance I felt like a naughty schoolgirl and loved every moment of it. No-one questioned us and when the gates opened we were literally the first to enter. We ran to the front of the stage like teenagers, giggling and breathless. Grinning from ear to ear we settled down to wait for the concert to begin several hours later. It was one of the best nights of my life, made so special because I shared it with my partner in crime, my bestie. If you were there that night and a couple of women, who were old enough to know better, jumped the queue in front of you, I apologise but I'm not sorry that we did it. I have held this fond memory for many years and will do so for many years to come.

One year Sue was given a large tent and wanted to erect it to see if it was all intact. Her garden was smaller than ours so she asked if we could put it up at our house. We did and it stayed there all summer, the children had so much fun in it. They had parties, sleepovers and endless hours of enjoyment in that tent.

There's a valuable lesson in all of this, it is more often than not the free and simple things in life that children get real pleasure from, and the greatest gift you can give them is your time and love. Like the days we used to go to the beach with my good friend Pip and her children. We would pack everything we needed for the day, including a picnic, then head off to an area where there was nothing but sand and the ocean. I have no doubt that if you asked the children to this day they would say these were some of their happiest childhood memories.

Pip and I also took the children on holiday to Cornwall one year, to stay in her aunt's caravan. Every day was spent walking through the woods to the beach, armed as always with everything we could possibly need for the day. The children would play beautifully together, we swam in the sea, scoured the beach for shells, discovered the coves and built sandcastles. Almost 30 years later I can still remember every detail of that holiday as if it were yesterday and the children, now parents themselves, still talk of their memories in Cornwall with fondness.

The funniest memory Pip and I have of our Cornish holiday is of the day we walked to the beach through the woods. Aaron and Pip's son, Luke, refused to put their shoes on so we warned them that it would get uncomfortable and that if it did then we didn't want to hear the whingeing, they'd been warned. On the way back the boys had been charged with carrying our bag of rubbish and the complaining about their feet hurting started up, as we knew it would. Simultaneously Pip and I nipped it in the bud, they had made their choice and would have to deal with it.

F*ck the Biscuits

It went quiet, that seemed a little too easy. We looked round to find that they had used empty crisp packets as makeshift shoes which were obviously working. We all found it absolutely hilarious, and totally admired their initiative. Many years later, when the children were young adults, Pip got married and a hen weekend was arranged for her at a local spa. We were to play a game whereby the guests would take her a present which had to be something that would be a clue for her to guess who had gifted the item. That was how I came to give a dear friend two empty crisp packets and a cornish pasty for her wedding present!

I found it incredibly hard to be a single mother, not so much the practicalities but more the emotional aspect, and the constant struggle to be both mum and dad. I wanted Aaron to have what I considered to be a normal family life, in particular a brother or sister, and felt for many years that my poor life choices had deprived him of that opportunity. Bringing up a child in any situation is difficult, and being a single parent adds to the stress and pressure. I did my best with what I had but there were times when I got it monumentally wrong. More so in my own personal life which inevitably had an impact on Aaron's home life. Looking back I can see now how vulnerable I was, and that I went from one unsuitable relationship to another in search of stability and security for us both. I don't know how I would have coped without my friends, and the support from my mum who lived in the same village and played a significant part in Aaron's upbringing. He would regularly ride his bike to visit her, staying for his tea and having a look to see what was in 'Garfield'. This was a biscuit barrel in the shape of Garfield the cat which, along with his favourite cookies, would also have some pocket money inside. He was extremely close to his Nanny, he loved her dearly, and the first time his heart was broken was when she died from cancer. He was only seventeen years old.

Aaron was a good child, he had such a warm and open heart and was kind and loving. He still is. I often look back with fond memories at the day we went out to buy a bag of coal. I started to carry it from the car but Aaron insisted on helping me, he wouldn't take no for an answer. As I watched my little boy struggle to carry the heavy sack, which was nearly as big as him, tears welled in my eyes. This little one was so determined to help his mum, it mattered so much to him, when push came to shove it was the two of us against the world. He was funny too, mischievous and popular - kids wanted to be around him and he had a smile that could warm any adult's heart. I was a proud mum. He would always stand up for the underdog and was absolutely fearless.

By the time he was halfway through secondary school he'd been to A & E more times than most people do in a lifetime. He could never see the danger in anything, and although he may have matured over the years, he's still pretty fearless to this day. I'm not sure how old Aaron was when he made me breakfast in bed one Mother's Day. He was old enough to use the cooker, but certainly not old enough to do it very well. I woke to the sound of him calling up the stairs, "Close your eyes, mum, I've got a surprise for you!" It was more of a shock than a surprise, there was a dinner plate piled high with food. I feigned delight, I'm not big on eating first thing in the morning at the best of times, but my joy in the effort he had made just for me was genuine. I felt like the richest woman in the world in that moment. It was pretty disgusting though, I can't lie. He explained that he couldn't find any sausages so he used fish fingers instead, a whole damned packet it would seem, and they were completely frozen in the middle. A testament to my love and devotion, I pretty much ate it all and it made me feel queasy all day. How could I resist that face full of anticipation as he watched me slowly devour the food he had so lovingly prepared, unaware that I secretly hoped he would disappear just long enough for me to hide it somewhere. Nevertheless it was such a touching and thoughtful thing to do and so typical of Aaron.

My father passed away when Aaron was a baby after seven long years of illness. He loved Aaron and was so proud of him. All the males on my father's side of the family have Edward in their name and we followed in the family tradition. My dad always referred to Aaron as 'his little Ted'. Time was precious and we were blessed that my dad got to meet, and spend some time with, his first grandson. Dad was an entrepreneur and businessman, he was not afraid to take risks and one of his many mottos was: "You can't lead your life with the handbrake on!" If there was a way to make a buck, my dad would find it.

My Mum and I took Aaron to the village fete when he was probably about six or seven years old, then after a while we realised he'd disappeared. We eventually found him behind the cricket pavilion, he had spent his 50p pocket money on a second-hand game and was charging the children 20p a go on it, he had made a tidy profit. As we stood watching and smiling my mum said, "That boy is just like your father, he'll always be able to make money". She was right, and when I look at the man he is today I am often reminded of my late dad, and I know just how proud he would be.

Despite the hassle the little creature caused me, I was really quite fond of Aaron's hamster, Honey. As kids do, he begged and pleaded for a hamster and made promises that he would lovingly care for it, feed and water it and clean the cage once a week. Yeah right. Mummy gave in to his pleas, then spent the next four years on hamster duty. There was one incident when it escaped up a pipe into the loft, and on numerous occasions it would manage to free itself from the cage and make its way into the hallway in full view of our cat, and it was almost impossible to catch the damn thing. I even had to cut it out of the back of the sofa when it ran off Aaron's lap and somehow ended up inside the fabric. It goes without saying that it was me who cleaned her cage and took care of her needs for the most part.

Apparently, pet hamsters live for about three years, I know this because I asked a little too often at work about their average lifespan, I was hamstered out! I thought Honey was invincible until I heard a voice shouting down the stairs one morning, "Mum, Honey won't wake up!" Oh dear, Honey had indeed gone over the rainbow... Aaron was so upset. We found a suitable box where he gently placed her on a bed of cotton wool, set some of her toys next to her and wrote 'I love you Honey' on the lid. We stood hand in hand at her graveside at the bottom of the garden in quiet contemplation. It was these little moments that Aaron and I shared over the years that bonded us so completely.

I was never one of those mums who was creative and certainly didn't excel at the school events. Not me, I was always willing to give things a go and tap into my domestic and creative side, but usually failed miserably. Aaron was to take part in a school play as one of several elephants. The parents were asked to provide a pair of grey woollen tights with an elephant's tail attached, what could possibly go wrong? For some reason I thought it was a great idea to cut the leg off of a spare pair of tights and stuff it to within an inch of its life before attaching it to the grey tights that he would be wearing. Feeling chuffed with myself I sent him off to school the following day with his costume, looking forward to going to see the play later that afternoon. A group of us mums were sitting waiting in the school hall for our little elephants to make their debut, as they walked on stage my heart momentarily stopped and my jaw dropped. All the children had little tails hanging down but Aaron had this enormous rigid thing sticking out at the back, nearly taking the others

The Two of Us Against the World

out with it. I was mortified but my mates thought it was utterly hilarious, one had to leave the hall because she couldn't control her laughter. For years I was the butt of the joke about the day Aaron had his trunk sticking out of his backside!

I have such wonderful memories of Aaron's childhood despite the struggles, we had a lot of happy times over the years. I watched him grow, fought his battles, wiped his tears and kept him safe. I always loved the end of the day when we were alone, bedtime cuddles and stories meant as much to me as it did to him. We were a team, just the two of us.

Unfortunately the teenage years brought their fair share of problems and challenges. There were aspects that I enjoyed in his early teens. I've always appreciated schoolboy humour and his friends used to make me laugh, I liked their company. We often had a house full of teenage lads and their trainers to trip over on a regular basis, all giggling and making mischief, and all with that distinct smell of testosterone! But like so many youngsters, Aaron was easily led and by the time he was in his late teens he'd got himself into some scrapes and his fair share of trouble. I once read Richard Branson's biography in which his father said he always knew that Richard would either end up in prison or as a millionaire. I could relate to this statement, Aaron was the same.

Those years were hard, I didn't always trust Aaron's judgement but he was at an age where I had no choice but to let him loose in the big wide world. Inevitably this led to a breakdown in communication between us and, to be honest, that bothered me more than anything. We'd always been so close, so to witness the demise of this relationship hurt me deeply. I understood it then, as I still do. Aaron was the victim of a broken home and there was nothing I could do to make that any different, but I never stopped believing in him. I never have. It was difficult and frustrating to see him behaving like this and not letting people see the amazing young man that lay beneath this facade. I would also worry about his emotional well-being, why did he go into self-destruct mode? What was going on beneath the surface?

The Two of Us Against the World

In truth I have to take responsibility for it all. I tried so hard over the years to be the best mum I could but there had been times when I had let him down, I made some poor decisions that, in the long term, were not in Aaron's best interest. However, I can honestly say from the bottom of my heart that, whilst being a single mum is the hardest thing I have ever done, it is also the most empowering and rewarding.

I lived in our lovely little home for the next thirty years. Out of the blue our lives took a dramatic turn, and everything changed in the course of one night. Aaron walked out of the house one evening when he was twenty-one years old, never to live there again.

CHAPTER TWO

The Night My Life Changed Forever

The weekend of 19th September 2008 was spent in Amsterdam with a group of girlfriends. It was my hen weekend. I was due to marry for the second time a few weeks later.

One of the girls with us that weekend was Olivia, my son's girlfriend of many years. Aaron was twenty-one years old at the time and Olivia a few years younger. Let me be honest here: Olivia and I had never really seen eye to eye and looking back I don't entirely know why. We simply didn't click. But she was my son's girlfriend and it seemed only right that she joined us. She was also the younger sister of Aaron's best friend of six years, Jack. In fact, that was how he and Olivia met. Olivia and Jack would both be coming to the wedding, or so we thought.

F*ck the Biscuits

The weekend was as much fun as we hoped it would be, we were a group of eight women who embraced everything that Amsterdam has to offer. Some go there for the tulips, not us. We were there to check out the coffee shop menus! To enlighten those of you who don't know, the coffee shop menus consist of various strengths of legal marijuana and we tried them all. I belly laughed for the entire weekend, to say the atmosphere was relaxed is an enormous understatement.

We all shared one dormitory and on the Sunday morning Olivia was sitting in her bed, still in her pyjamas, talking to Aaron on the phone. Her face was lit up and as I watched her I started to see her in a different light. I saw a kind, sweet, innocent girl who was clearly in love. I felt a warmth towards her that I'd never felt before. Then a voice in my head told me firmly to open up to her, talk to her and tell her that she was a good girl, that I was fond of her and pleased that she and Aaron had each other - so I did. I sat next to her and opened my heart.

The Night My Life Changed Forever

No-one could possibly have imagined that the following day she would be dead.

We travelled home on the Monday. It was the 22nd September 2008, a date that will forever be etched in my mind. It was also Jack's birthday so the three of them had decided to go out for a drink, then they planned to get a takeaway and go back to Olivia and Jack's home where they lived with their mum, Heather. They left me lying on the sofa feeling very delicate after the weekend, and laughing at my expense. Off they went, youngsters loving life.

It was just after midnight when my phone rang, I answered it sleepily and a voice screamed at me, "They're dead, they're dead!" It was Heather, and she was absolutely hysterical. I didn't want to listen to anything she was saying, so I thrust the phone at my fiancé, Mark.

My first, only and overwhelming thought was, "Do not tell me!" I jumped out of bed and started walking down the stairs, I had to get away. In my head all I could focus on was: "If anyone tells me Aaron is dead then he will be, if they don't tell me then it won't be true." I could hear Mark talking but refused to listen to anything he was saying. He followed me down the stairs, but I kept shouting, "No, don't tell me!" and made my way through the house, running away from him. Running away from the words that would mean my son was dead, and furious that Mark couldn't understand that it was imperative for him not to utter those words. It was literally a matter of life or death.

I was fleeing barefoot down the street when Mark shouted, "Aaron is alive!". I stopped. Now I was ready to listen.

He caught up with me and explained that there had been a fatal crash in which both Olivia and Jack had been killed, Aaron was the only survivor and we were to meet him at Colchester A&E. It transpired that Mark had been talking to the police who had taken the phone away from Heather. They were not aware that she had called me, they apologised that we had been informed in this way and told Mark that a police car was on its way to us but not to wait now that we knew, but to make our way directly to the hospital instead.

The Night My Life Changed Forever

Sitting on the edge of my bed, I knew I had to get dressed as quickly as possible to get to the hospital but I couldn't move, every limb felt heavy and lifeless. I was so scared. I desperately wanted to turn back time and be back in bed sleeping peacefully where this nightmare wasn't happening. I phoned my dear, lifelong friend, Sue. Despite her own fear and emotions, she calmly talked me through the actions I needed to take. She told me to just take one step at a time and to only deal with what is happening in the moment, and all I had to do then was to get dressed and get in the car. I will be forever grateful for her love, wisdom and guidance. I cannot imagine how I would have coped that night without her. On the way to the hospital I had a sudden and frightening thought - what if they have got it wrong and Aaron was not the survivor? Mark explained that it could only be Aaron because the one who survived had his leg in a cast. Aaron had broken his leg playing football a week or so previously, and his cast was a means of identifying which one of them had survived.

F*ck the Biscuits

I can never know how that night must have felt for Heather. The police traced Olivia's car to her house, and had to ask Heather who would have been driving the vehicle. She told them it was her daughter at which point they spoke the words that no-one ever wants to hear.... "Then I'm sorry to have to tell you...." They then asked who would have been in the passenger seat, she told them it would have been Aaron. They asked her who the passenger in the back of the car was and what he would have been wearing. She told them it was her son, Jack. You see, Olivia's car was a three door Audi so Aaron was a front seat passenger all the time his leg was broken because it was extremely difficult for him to climb into the back. The police then asked her to confirm it was Jack wearing a cast, at this point they had to tell her and repeat those words... "I'm sorry to have to tell you..."

I cannot even begin to know how she must have felt to be told that neither of her children in the car had survived. At some point during this nightmare I had an honest, open and heartbreaking conversation with Heather when we both confessed the momentary but overwhelming feeling of relief, bordering on delight, that it was someone else's child who had been killed. In Heather's case she was wrong. I could never envisage her pain, and I never will.

An extraordinary thing had happened that night. On the way home they had stopped to pick up a takeaway. Aaron was waiting for Jack by the car for him to get in the back, he waited some while in the cold until a voice in his head told him clearly to get in the back of the car. Aaron felt compelled to follow the instruction and somehow struggled onto the back seat, not knowing then that it would be the very thing that would save his life.

We arrived at A&E. I didn't imagine the hospital car park would be so quiet and calm, almost eerily quiet. Maybe it just felt that way in comparison with the chaos in my head. As we approached the entrance I saw her... a female police officer was heading towards me. Anger started to build up inside me: now this bloody woman was going to tell me that my son was dead. What part of "Don't tell me!" don't these people understand?! She cannot make it true, I won't let her.

F*ck the Biscuits

As she walked towards me, I started to say "No, don't say anything!" She kept coming towards me as I started to back away, by this time shouting at her not to tell me. Her pace quickened and, as she caught up with me, I was about to push her away but she grabbed me before I could do anything. By then I was fuelled by anger and tried to lash out, she held me tightly, looked me in the face and said firmly but with genuine kindness, "From a mum to a mum, I'm telling you he's calling for you now, come with me". The anger turned to overwhelming relief. I went from hating this woman to needing her in an instant, she was a mum too and she didn't tell me that Aaron was dead, that was good enough for me so now I trusted her.

Mark and I followed her into the hospital, she took us straight to a room where the registrar and consultant were waiting for us. As I mentioned earlier, Aaron was a fearless child so I'd been to A&E several times over the years and it had always been a challenge just to get to talk to anyone, let alone the top guys, so I knew this was serious. Something about it felt surreal - like this wasn't really happening to me, I was an outsider looking in. The consultant explained that Aaron had broken his spine, he was paralysed and had experienced some seizures so they suspected head injuries. We were also told that the others were found dead at the scene.

The team went on to tell us their plan of action, but by that point they may as well have been telling me that after his next scan we'd all be going on a teddy bears picnic! My brain wasn't even beginning to compute the phrase 'broken spine', and absolutely nothing else seemed to be making any sense to me. I was switching off, shutting down... all I could think was "Let me see my son, so I can make him better".

But I couldn't fix him, I couldn't make him better, and I couldn't make this go away. Although I didn't know it at the time, the feeling of sheer helplessness I felt sitting at Aaron's bedside that night would only escalate over the coming months.

My heart was racing when the nurses took me to him, I didn't know what to expect and every worst case scenario raced through my mind in the short time it took to walk to the emergency room. Aaron reached his arms out to me, and we simply held each other tight. Inevitably he kept asking what had happened to Olivia and Jack, I was mute. I just couldn't bring myself to tell him, though the look in his eyes told me he already knew the truth. He was clinging on to the hope that he'd got it wrong, and the hospital had managed to save them.

The doctors were anxious for Aaron to have another CT scan so it was decided to take him straight to radiology and then when he was back they would join us and tell us 'together' what had become of Olivia and Jack. As they wheeled his bed down the corridor, he called out to me: "Mum, I'm paralysed!" The look of despair in his eyes will forever haunt me, this was the first time I heard and understood the enormity of those words - they stabbed me in my heart and rebounded round and round in my head. He disappeared from sight and I was left standing there, rooted to the spot. My whole world changed in that moment.

As agreed, when he returned from the scan, I told Aaron I would get the doctors to come and tell us what had happened to the others. When they told us, Aaron let out a deep, primal scream of pure pain and all I could do was cry while I cradled him in my arms. I had heard that scream once before, it was the same noise my mother made the day my sister was cremated many years previously. That's what intense pain sounds like. I could never forget it.

The scan revealed that Aaron's spine was dislocated at L1/T12 (lumbar and thoracic sections), one vertebra was badly damaged and a shard of bone was pressing against the spinal cord. One false move and it was game over.

The medical team decided to transfer him to Queen's Hospital in Romford which has a specialist neuroscience centre and was much better equipped to deal with Aaron's injury. He was to be flown there by helicopter as this was the safest and fastest way, avoiding any jarring that could cause the sharp bone to tear his spinal cord. We had to wait until morning because the Air Ambulance was not allowed to fly in darkness. Just before he was due to leave Aaron took my hand and said, "Mum, I'm scared, will you come with me?"

Now, this might be a good time to mention that I have one real phobia.... You've guessed it - heights! Flying in a helicopter was my absolute worst fear. Just then my knight in shining armour – well, a doctor in a red boiler suit, to be precise - walked in with the kindest of smiles and explained that there was no room for anyone else on board. Dilemma averted. He also completely reassured Aaron that he had plenty of painkillers on board and that he would be perfectly safe in his hands. I never saw this man again but my gratitude for his compassion and professionalism remains to this day.

Not long after arriving at A&E I had phoned Steve, Aaron's dad, to tell him what was happening. The police had - understandably but incorrectly - assumed that Mark was Aaron's father which is why it had been up to me to call Steve that night. He arrived shortly afterwards and stayed with us throughout the night, along with his wife, Cathy, both of whom would go on to play an integral part in Aaron's recovery. Before the Air Ambulance left, Steve had gone on ahead to meet Aaron upon his arrival in Romford.

After what seemed like an eternity, the helicopter took off and was on its way. I was left standing by the heliport feeling like a mother whose newborn had been ripped from her arms. I fell to my knees and wept. My baby had been taken from me, just when he needed me the most. When I emerged from this ugly cry - and it was ugly, you know the one.... face crumpled, snot and tears everywhere - I saw Mark just standing there looking somewhat dazed. He never did become comfortable with the ugly cries that would follow for years to come. I vaguely remember there being someone else nearby desperately trying to look calm and acting as though a broken woman on her knees was the norm, nothing to see here!

My first recollection of Romford Hospital was being led into the Intensive Care unit and seeing Aaron lying on his bed pretty out of it. He had been sedated. There were some seriously ill patients in the unit and it was a scary place. The nursing staff were super busy and I remember there being a lot of police around. That was when we met the female officer in charge of the investigation into the cause of the crash, and I believe she was also a family support officer. She briefly introduced herself to me and gave me her contact details, she also told me that Aaron had been wearing his seatbelt at the time of the accident and that she would have a report and all relevant details ready for the insurance claim as soon as possible, she advised not to worry about it until we were settled but that I should give it careful consideration as soon as I could. Insurance claim? The concept hadn't even entered my head but as it turned out it was a blessing that someone had the foresight to consider it.

I don't know at what point my little breakdown in Intensive Care happened. Everything seemed to be a blur, a frenzy of people, noises yet silence. I didn't know where to turn or what to do and felt like I just couldn't take it anymore, I wanted to run away and hide. I've no doubt the fact that I hadn't actually been to bed or slept for some time didn't help either. The next thing I knew the Sister in charge took me by the

The Night My Life Changed Forever

arm and led me into her office. Apparently I had been standing in the middle of the ward trembling with tears streaming down my face, doubtless that was why everything was a blur, I clearly recall not being able to see anything properly. The Sister was so kind, she sat me down and I told her what had happened thus far. Surprisingly, she was not aware that Aaron was the sole survivor of the accident and clearly hadn't been updated on a lot of details. She showed me to a room with a guest bed in it and told me I had to rest, to get my head down because I was going to need my strength. She wasn't kidding. Not surprisingly I didn't sleep... not for several more days as it turned out. If I was to be of any help and any kind of support to Aaron, I seriously needed to get my shit together!

Visiting in the Intensive Care ward was for next of kin only, so Steve and I were working on a rota system to be at Aaron's bedside at all times. The first time I emerged from the ward, I made my way down the stairs to the ground floor - the hospital seemed absolutely huge, like a big shopping precinct. I was stunned when I walked into the cafe, there sat some

F*ck the Biscuits

family and friends. I had no idea they were there, they knew they couldn't get to see Aaron but were waiting in the wings to support in any way they could. They will never know how much that meant to me. It blew my mind and it was the first of so many times that I truly felt the power of love.

CHAPTER THREE

Pioneering Surgery

A few days later I was persuaded to go home to get a shower and a change of clothes at the very least. I suspect that was more for other people's benefit than my own, I doubt being too close to me was a particularly pleasant experience by then. I was exhausted. I mean totally, utterly and completely exhausted. I didn't want to go home, to go to bed, or do anything other than be at the hospital with Aaron.

It's funny how us mums think we're indispensable, did I assume that the team of highly trained professionals couldn't manage without me? No, but Aaron needed me, I was his mother, it's that simple. The bubble of the Intensive Care unit, holding Aaron's hand, had a feeling of safety. The outside world felt alien, as if I had no place there anymore.

Before going home, I called in to see Sue. She lived two doors down from me, was my best friend of twenty years or so, and I hadn't seen her since I called her on the night of the accident. She opened the door and we simply fell into each other's arms, not much was said. What was there to say? Sue had been the one to organise my hen weekend in Amsterdam and, as well as being fraught with worry for Aaron and me, she was - along with us all - feeling traumatised and grieving the loss of Olivia and Jack. Particularly Olivia with whom she had formed a bond that weekend.

When I eventually got home I walked into the lounge, sat on the sofa and sobbed, reality was slowly sinking in and I cried until there were no more tears left to shed. Most women will understand when I say that men mean well but, when we have a good old cry, most have this caveman-like instinct to fix everything. Whether he just knew that this was beyond fixing I don't know, but Mark's reaction was pretty spot on. He brought me tea and tissues and left me to weep until I ran out of tears and ran out of energy.

From then on I would come home late from the hospital every night, always exhausted and always fraught with anxiety. What if Aaron woke in the night feeling frightened or in pain and needed me? How was he coping with his grief? How would he continue to cope with his grief, would he ever get over this? How was Heather, did she have a good support network to help her through the days? So many thoughts running endlessly through my mind, it was constant and draining. Finally falling asleep was a small respite, as was that brief moment when you wake and just for a second you have forgotten everything that's happening. That split second was my favourite part of the day and the only letup my mind was afforded.

I did have a day when I took a break from the hospital, Cathy told me to stay at home and said that she would be mum that day. I am so grateful for her support, and she was right. I needed a day to take care of things at home. Our lives as we knew them had come to an abrupt end and I needed to take care of some practicalities. There was an enormous amount of telephone messages to respond to, post to take care of and, if this was going to work, I needed to recruit friends and family to take care of my life while I took care of Aaron. I worked my way through an overwhelming 'to do' list that day, taking a break every now and then to weep. We had a long way to go and yet already I felt as though I had run out of energy, feeling weak and powerless. I knew that I needed to get my act together pretty sharpish. The pressure and responsibility felt all consuming.

I thought about Heather every day, my heart went out to her but there was nothing I could do to take away her agony. I also knew I should go and see her, it was the least I could do. It wasn't just a sense of duty though, we had a bond. Word of the accident had got round, it was in the papers and on the news. Everyone was talking about 'that terrible accident', Heather and I were 'those poor mums' that others were talking about. What a tragedy it was that connected us.

As I pulled up outside her house my heart was racing, I was shaking and I felt sick. I can't deny it was tempting to just drive off, put this off for another day. But I couldn't bury my head in the sand, this was all part of the reality of my life now. My biggest fear was that she would hate me, my son had lived when two of her children had been killed. Would she resent me for that? The door was answered by a friend who took me through to the kitchen where Heather was sitting. As I walked in, she slowly got up and walked towards me, our eyes met and we looked at each other for what seemed like an eternity. Nothing was spoken yet everything was said. Then she fell into my arms and we both sobbed, holding each other tightly. Eventually we broke apart, our tears combined made our faces and clothes wet.

Then we talked, comfortably and openly. She told me all about that fateful night, the police turning up at her house and the sequence of events that followed. I had a small insight into her world of pain when she told me that the following day she was so weak that she could barely stand, so her best friend had stripped them both naked and taken her into the shower, held her up and washed her. That's friendship at its deepest and purest. Thank God she had that friend to care for her.

I had taken a bunch of flowers with me but she told me that she didn't want them in the house so she suggested we take them together to lay at the scene of the accident. I didn't feel anywhere near ready to go there, but if Heather could do this then so could I. Although there was an incredible amount of flowers all laid neatly, the only thing I could see when we arrived was the image of the car upside down with Aaron inside screaming. Shutting my eyes didn't make it go away. I got flashes of blue lights in darkness, of how Jack and Olivia must have looked as they lay dead in the vehicle. I pictured Aaron's face, the anguish and fear. This was too much, I just wanted to run and never stop. The accident took place at the end of a bridge that crosses the A12 near Colchester and still to this day I shudder as I drive underneath it, and I don't believe that will ever change.

It's a cliche I know but it's absolutely true to say that at times like this you really value friendship and kindness. Endless messages of support were being sent to us - cards, flowers, telephone messages. Even people I didn't know particularly well were reaching out.

This may be a good time to talk about the support we received throughout this journey. We quickly set up a system to update everyone, all I had to do was send one message to a nominated friend who would in turn update everyone else. This was in the good old days before WhatsApp, remember. I was bowled over by the words of love and encouragement, and all the offers of help with practical things too. It wasn't all bad, at least I didn't have to do my own washing and ironing for a while!

Of course, there were close friends and family, and without them I honestly don't think I would have coped, but love and support also came in ways I least expected. At the time we lived in the village where I grew up and where I subsequently raised Aaron. The community pulled together in ways I would never have envisaged. Flowers left on my doorstep, food parcels, poems, letters, cards. Love comes in many guises. Neighbours had keys to my house so sometimes I would find home-cooked food in the fridge or a pile of fresh laundry on the table. Aaron's old headmaster wrote him a long letter, filled with love and encouragement. There were times when I would lay in bed at night and literally feel the love that surrounded me. It enveloped me.

Not one small act of kindness went unnoticed. It also came to my attention that the local church had set up a prayer group for him and prayed for his recovery and for my strength on a regular basis. We're not regular churchgoers so I was both surprised and touched that they would do this for us. I later learned that other church groups in neighbouring villages had heard about Aaron's accident and were doing the same. To be honest there were times when it got too much, I couldn't quickly pop to the local shop any more, that's for certain. It could take over an hour to buy a box of teabags! Offers of financial help came in too, and were both gratefully and graciously received. Mark was self-employed and wasn't always available to work, Aaron and I no longer had an income so the whole thing did take its toll financially.

It was a week before Aaron had his surgery at Queen's Hospital in Romford to realign his spine. There were two reasons for the delay. Firstly, his body was still in shock and he needed time for his system to rest and recuperate before putting it through any more trauma. Secondly, they didn't entirely know what to do. The

Pioneering Surgery

positioning of the dislocated vertebrae, along with the fact that one of them was completely shattered, was a unique injury and they'd never come across this before. The consultant, a neurosurgeon by the name of Mr David, and his team literally had to come up with a plan. They did a few 'trial runs' first, this was pioneering surgery.

The day of the surgery came. Steve and I went as far as the operating theatre with Aaron and were able to stay with him while they gave him his anaesthetic. You would probably, understandably, assume that this was a traumatic time for me, yet surprisingly it wasn't. I grant you it wasn't exactly a pleasant experience but I somehow had this inner faith in the surgeons, in the process and saw it as a means to fix my baby - to make him all better. "Everything will be okay now..."

I was naive enough to believe that once this operation was over and he recovered from it our lives would return to normal. How wrong was I?

It was Steve who didn't fare too well at this point, he broke down outside the theatre and wept in my arms.

F*ck the Biscuits

Steve and I eventually made our way back down to the cafe where our respective partners were sitting patiently, then went our separate ways to start the long waiting game. I don't know what Steve and Cathy did to kill time during Aaron's gruelling eight-hour operation, but the first thing I did was eat. I'd hardly eaten anything since this ordeal began, just enough to fulfil basic needs. Now I was hungry - bizarre, I know. I felt a certain sense of reassurance that Aaron was in good hands and his body was finally being repaired. At long last I could relax. I ate a huge breakfast and enjoyed every mouthful. I very much doubt anyone in that cafe would have guessed that my only son was having pioneering surgery on his spine at that moment as they watched me tuck in.

The day passed slowly after that, but eventually Steve and I got the call to say Aaron was in recovery and we could go and see him. As we made our way there, I psyched myself up ready for the worst. I imagined Aaron would look pale and very weak and be quite unresponsive. I got that wrong too. He looked a picture of health, he had colour in his cheeks and a beaming smile on his face.

We accompanied the staff who wheeled him back to Intensive Care and as we made our way down the corridor Aaron started giggling, he was acting very strange. Then he got loud, too loud. He was laughing and shouting at the top of his voice, babbling about chickens! Yup, had we heard the joke about chickens? Did anyone really know what came first, the chicken or the egg? Did anyone care? It was equal parts embarrassing and hilarious. Steve and I looked at each other bemused, then laughed. This was a light-hearted moment in an otherwise dark time in our lives so we made the most of it.

We all had to try and calm him down before going onto the ward. There were some very sick patients in the unit who doubtless wouldn't see the funny side, although I have to admit it was quite amusing. This day was becoming more surreal by the minute. It transpired that the reason Aaron looked so healthy was because he'd had a blood transfusion and the reason he was behaving as if he'd had far too many pints was because he was high on a cocktail of drugs.

Later that day I remember joining Steve briefly in the consultant's office. Steve had already met with them and told me that they had assured him the surgery went well, and had explained to him that they had used titanium rods to realign and secure Aaron's spine, that the membrane of the spinal cord had been torn which they were able to repair, and that he had lost some spinal fluid. I had no questions to ask in the office, I was happy to let Steve deal with this. I just wanted to be mum and be at Aaron's side.

This turned out to be an absolute blessing. When we left the office Steve went on to tell me that it all went well and that, although Aaron was paralysed for now, with a lot of hard work and determination he would over time recover from the paralysis and learn to walk again. Aaron would be transferred to a specialist spinal unit as soon as a place was available for physiotherapy and his journey to recovery would begin. I was elated, the relief was all consuming. That evening I was talking to one of Aaron's friends on the phone, telling him the good news. When I looked round I saw Mark crying and recall wondering why he was so upset when today had been such a success. I just assumed he was overwhelmed with emotion, I knew that one.

The days passed, each with a new challenge. The reprieve from the anguish didn't last long. I quickly realised that this was going to be a long road to recovery, and there was a niggling doubt in the back of my mind. None of the medical staff mentioned his prognosis, there was an underlying feeling that things weren't quite as they seemed. I chose not to deal with it or question anything, I now realise that subconsciously I knew that this was far worse than Steve was letting on but my mind couldn't cope with any more heartache at this point so I chose to ignore my instinct.

I would spend every day at the hospital in the unit with Aaron and return home each night. The journey back and forth wasn't easy. The hospital was about an hour's drive from home, I was too tired and delicate to be able to drive myself. It was usually Mark that came with me but sometimes friends or family would take me.

I was in the car while Sue was driving one day when I suddenly confessed to her that I was absolutely terrified of being on the road. Aaron's accident had occurred at 70 miles an hour, and I was petrified that the same thing would happen to me. Not for selfish reasons, I didn't care about my own wellbeing, but how would Aaron cope if on top of everything else I were to be involved in a serious car crash too? I realise that's completely irrational thinking but what was going on in my life at the time was hardly conducive to any logical thought processes. Sue could see my anxiety and, as always, kept calm and told me it was perfectly understandable to feel that way. She slowed down, drove perfectly and didn't judge me. Love her.

Aaron called me one night, in the early hours of the morning. He was crying and screaming, telling me about a nurse who was cruel and hurting him. He begged me to help. Apparently she was attempting to give him an injection in the back of his hand and something had gone wrong causing his hand to swell considerably. I kept Aaron talking and asked Mark to phone the ward to find out what on earth was going on. While I was talking to Aaron, the Sister in charge came in. I could hear her talking kindly to Aaron, she calmed him down and presumably resolved the problem.

Aaron may have been twenty-one years old but he was broken physically and mentally and he was my little boy. When I couldn't be with him, I needed to know he was in the best hands of people who cared deeply about his welfare. Although this was an unfortunate and isolated incident, it unnerved me and from that time on I could never leave the hospital knowing that he would be okay for the relatively short period of time I couldn't be there. The anguish was relentless.

No-one warns you about the loneliness. There were times throughout this entire ordeal when I felt a deep-rooted sense of isolation. It's easy to feel as though you're the only person going through this ordeal, it's uncharted territory so each day, each incident, each conversation is a learning curve. One of these moments of isolation happened when I was having a coffee in the hospital cafe. It was really busy and a hive of activity and yet I felt like the only person there, an outsider to the real world. I desperately wanted to be in the arms of my friends, to feel safe.

A few days later I spoke to another dear and lifelong friend, Jan, and told her how I had felt and that I couldn't call her because to talk to her and know that she was not there with me to console me would be too much to bear. Her answer was simple and touched my heart. She softly said "How do you know I wouldn't have been there? I'd have come." Wow. I felt her love then, just as I do to this day.

Jan and I met a long time ago, and bonded on a girls' trip to Turkey. Just like my relationship with Sue, we totally understand each other. She is my soulmate, and has been a pivotal part of my emotional and spiritual journey. We have walked miles and miles over the years with our respective dogs, basking in nature. These walks are truly meditative. It was Jan who taught me an incredibly valuable lesson - to see and appreciate nature in all its glory, and to notice every small detail. She sees the pollen sacks on a bee, the patterns in a butterfly wing, the delicacy of a small petal. Jan makes the ordinary come alive. It was when we were out walking one day that she mentioned how she wished she could draw and paint, in response to which I asked her how she knew she couldn't. Since that day she has gone on to produce some stunning pieces of art, from paintings to ceramics and lots more. She is truly talented and I am so proud to witness her creative journey as it unfolds. Time spent with Jan is always uplifting. She is gentle, kind and wise. My cheerleader. And if hugging was an Olympic sport she would win gold, Jan hugs with her heart. We have shared so much together from Gong Bath Meditation to spending a weekend at hers under the duvet with copious amounts of chocolate and wine binge watching Peter Kay, and everything in between.

My sister, Tracy, was an absolute rock too. She sat with me at Aaron's bedside one day. I was holding Aaron's hand and stroking his forehead as he was slowly drifting off to sleep. As I looked at him, I became overwhelmed with emotion, my eyes began to fill with tears and my heart felt like it would literally break under the strain. Tracy slowly reached forward, took Aaron's hand from mine and gently put it in hers, she started stroking his head and whispered to me to go and take a break. I thanked God for her then, as I do now.

Tracy and I had a privileged yet troubled upbringing. We were the youngest of four, with a considerable age gap between us and our older brother and sister. She was just a small child when our parents' marriage became so difficult that the arguments they had were often violent and disturbing. It was during these fights that I would go and get Tracy from her room, take her into my bedroom and lay her next to me. I would cover her ears in an attempt to block out what was happening and soothe her fears. In so many ways we have grown up to be very different people with different interests but the bond that we formed during those childhood adversities has never left us. We are always there to support each other and I love her dearly.

By this time Aaron had been at Romford Hospital for a few weeks. This nightmare had begun just after returning from my hen weekend - I was supposed to be getting married. Despite all the months, probably years, of preparation for the big day I completely forgot about it. Again, Sue to the rescue. She quietly approached me and said, "Babe, your wedding is next week. Do you have a folder?" (She knows me too well, there's always a folder!) "I'll take care of it." And she did, my girl is amazing. Everything was cancelled or postponed until further notice and we were given full refunds from everyone concerned. It was as if the wedding had never existed.

Her task was aided considerably by the fact that, by now, most people knew what had happened. The details of the accident had been all over the media. Aaron, Olivia and Jack were famous. It was ludicrous. This heartbreak was sensationalised on local television stations and was selling newspapers. Heather was being hassled by journalists to the point where the police got involved to protect her from this unnecessary pressure. A journalist knocked on my door too on the one odd occasion that I was at home, she was clearly very good at her job. She was kind, warm in her approach and I fell for it, hook, line and sinker. When the article appeared in the paper the next day, the police officer who had been looking after us was not amused. She contacted the newspaper office to let them know that they were to leave us alone and I never heard from them again. Until eventually I contacted them, but more about that later.

The reality of the situation and the grief was starting to kick in, especially for Aaron. He was distraught, unable to sleep and would phone his friends at all hours through the night. Each one of them gave him what he needed in that moment, for which I am indebted to them. His entire circle of friends was in shock, the grief impacting all these young people was painful to witness. They were scared, confused and hurting.

Aaron was linked up to a morphine drip which he was able to operate himself, when he felt pain from his injury and surgery he could simply press a button and this would automatically administer a shot of morphine. The problem was that this drug is highly addictive and was also helping him to shut his mind down to the intense grief and trauma. It stopped the emotional pain as well as the physical pain, and helped to take away the horrendous flashbacks. His medical team were becoming increasingly concerned, they spoke to me about it and I remember thinking, "I've got enough on my plate, what do you expect me to do about it?". My worry wasn't about the morphine, my worry was for Aaron's mental and emotional state. Just one more problem I couldn't solve for him. We were spared from the dilemma of knowing just how we were going to deal with this by the call to say a place had become available at Stoke Mandeville Spinal Unit and he would be transferred within a couple of days.

Shortly after that the ward Sister, a beautiful and caring soul by the name of Sister Miranda, came to talk to me. She told me that we had a long and arduous journey ahead and things would be tough, I would need to dig deep for courage and there might be times when Aaron would feel extreme anger and frustration. She gently reminded me that we often take things out on those we love the most so I must try to remain strong for him. There was something else she needed to say.... that if Aaron were to make any progress it was

F*ck the Biscuits

going to take everything he had, absolutely everything. She completely understood his grief but said that he needed to put that to one side for the time being, his legs had to become his best friends now.

I woke up to the gravity of the situation during that conversation. I got what she was saying but you're kidding me, right? I was there that night in A&E when his heart was ripped out and torn apart and now you honestly expect me to tell him to simply forget about them? Yet I knew she was right.

That night I went home and I prayed, and from then on I prayed every single night. I've always been a spiritual person though I don't have a religion. Yet I prayed that night and then every single night until my prayers were finally answered. It didn't matter how exhausted I was, I would light a candle and pray, frankly to any deity prepared to listen.

I kept it simple... Let Aaron walk again... Let Heather cope with her pain... and in return I promised to give something back.

Pioneering Surgery

As I knelt by my bed that night I also asked for guidance, should I tell Aaron what Sister Miranda had said? In all honesty, I wanted to bury my head in the sand and pretend the conversation had never taken place. But it had. I desperately needed to know whether to tell him and, if so, how to tell him. At that point a picture of Olivia's face started to emerge in my mind. It got closer and closer until it encompassed my entire vision, as if she were there in the room with me - her face almost touching mine. Then she firmly said, "Tell him, tell him" as if she were shouting an order at me. I was oblivious to everything else, all I could hear was her voice and all I could see was her face. I had my answer, but more importantly I had her blessing. I quietly thanked her and knew exactly what I had to do. The next day I sat with Aaron and told him not only what Sister Miranda had said, but what Olivia had told me too. I relayed my experience to him and he understood exactly what it meant, and that she had given him her blessing too.

A few days later we were told Aaron was being transferred to Stoke Mandeville that day. Finally, let's get this show on the road. The ambulance was prepared, bearing in mind it would take about an hour and a half to get there and Aaron was very sick. Just before he was put in the ambulance, Mr David's right hand man popped his head round the corner. He had come to wish Aaron farewell, as he left the bedside he looked Aaron directly in the face and said, "We've done what we can here, the rest is up to you" as he pointed to Aaron's head and gently tapped him on the temple. I doubt he could have known then how profound his words would turn out to be.

Mark and I were to follow in our car, Cathy in her car and Steve would ride in the ambulance. The convoy left the hospital heading for the unknown.

CHAPTER FOUR

And Still No-One Listens

Even the journey to Stoke Mandeville was harrowing. We had waited this long so I wasn't sure why the ambulance was in such a hurry to get there, yet it sped down the M25 leaving us struggling to keep up. We had no idea where we were going or what to expect when we got there. My little boy was in that ambulance and I couldn't lose him. There were brief times during the journey when I tried to distract myself and I'll have to confess it was quite amusing to watch Cathy's Mini swaying from lane to lane, determined not to let anything get between her and the ambulance. She looked as if she was being towed whilst hurtling down the motorway and had absolutely no control of the speed she was doing. But it wasn't long before the frightening reality kicked in. My heart and head were pounding and I couldn't wait to just get there. If I'd have known what was to follow maybe I wouldn't have been in such a rush.

Aaron was wheeled into a room where he was to be assessed before being taken to a ward. The tests were relentless and the process seemed to take forever. Steve and I stayed with Aaron while Mark and Cathy waited, yet again, in the wings. Very little was explained to us but it was obvious that the hospital staff were trying to ascertain how much feeling Aaron had from the waist down, just as it was obvious that the answer to that question was absolutely none.

It wasn't until now that I began to understand that paralysis is not just a matter of the legs not working, Aaron had absolutely no sensation in the lower half of his body. It freaked me out to watch them use a sharp instrument to prick his legs, bottom, hips and very private parts whilst all the time he was completely unaware of it. This was my first introduction to the complexity of spinal cord injury.

Endless blood tests were taken, and I could see Aaron becoming paler and paler. He told the doctors that he felt sick and dizzy, then I intervened and told them that I thought he was about to faint. That's okay they said, we've nearly finished. "No, it's bloody well not okay!" I thought to myself. Aaron drifted out of consciousness for a short time and I felt as though I just wanted to scoop him into my arms and run as far away as possible. I needed a break, to go and grab a coffee and get my head together. I turned to Steve to ask him if he would mind if I disappeared for a while but the look on his face gave me my answer. My ex-husband sat in a chair opposite me and he looked like a lost child, I could see he was terrified and emotionally he'd had enough. I couldn't leave him. I couldn't leave either of them.

Finally the doctors were finished and told us to wait, as the consultant would be with us shortly. By now Aaron had recovered a little and was feeling better. Eventually the door opened and there appeared Mr. Newton. He was one of the leading spinal injury specialists at the unit and was to be in charge of Aaron's case.

F*ck the Biscuits

What an extraordinary man. He reminded me a little of a mad scientist, in his white coat he would just appear from nowhere, he never seemed to walk into a room, he would just be there. We later learned that he used to be a priest but trained as a medical professional quite late in life because he had a calling to help people and make a difference. My kind of guy. He had a great energy about him, commanding yet gentle. He introduced himself and spoke to Aaron at length, asking him lots of questions about the accident and how he was feeling and explained to Aaron that he would have a team of specialists assigned to his case. Fantastic, I felt such a surge of relief. We were in safe hands, at last it started to feel okay.

Mr. Newton shook our hands to depart but just as he was about to walk away he turned to Aaron and said "You'll be fine, you have good upper body strength, you'll make a great paraplegic!". My heart literally stopped in that moment, then I felt a wave of shock pulse through my body, like my nervous system had been hit by a bolt of electricity. His words rushed over me like a hot wave. How bloody dare he? Paraplegic!

His words stung and I could feel the heat and anger rising in me. Bearing in mind that at this point Aaron and I were unaware of his prognosis, it was a cruel way to introduce us to this prospect. I rather suspect that Mr. Newton believed we had a greater understanding of the situation we faced. Nevertheless it was such a flippant, disrespectful and ultimately inhumane way to tell a patient, and their loved ones, that they might never walk again. It was Mr. Newton's way and I am sure he meant no harm. But harm it did. My mind was in chaos. I felt angry, confused and frightened.

Strangely the incident passed fairly quickly so after my initial reaction had subsided, I gave it little significance, assuming that once they got all of Aaron's medical records, he would realise the error of his judgement. I did wonder if I was the only person in the room who heard him, no-one else seemed to react and, in all honesty, Aaron seemed too dazed and traumatised to register what was going on. Or so I thought.

It was many years later that I heard the truth from Aaron as to how it really felt for him that day. He was utterly terrified. Although we had done all we could to comfort and shield him in the early days, he realised that, at twenty-one years old, he could be facing the rest of his life in a wheelchair. Knowing that he was being taken to Stoke Mandeville Spinal Unit gave him immense hope, this was where he was going to learn to walk again. He had an overwhelming sense at Romford Hospital that no-one was listening to him, not understanding how desperate he was to walk, or that he was going to walk again. All this while he had told himself not to worry, because when he got to the spinal unit, it would all change. His voice would be heard.

And now here he was lying weak, vulnerable and helpless - not even able to sit up - and the one person who could help him wasn't hearing him either. It wasn't that Aaron was too dazed to register what Mr. Newton had said, it was that all hope in that moment had been completely crushed and he had shut down, lost his will and had no desire to even be alive anymore.

CHAPTER FIVE

The Place Where Miracles Happen

For the next few weeks, Aaron stayed on an acute ward at Stoke Mandeville, and we got to know the spinal unit fairly well. It was a little while before other family members were able to visit, mainly because Aaron didn't yet feel ready to see anyone else. It was incredibly hard to watch Aaron facing the emotional and psychological trauma day in and day out. He had harrowing flashbacks of that fateful night, remembering with clarity every detail including laying in the wreckage amongst the silence of death. He knew then that he was the only one still alive. He would have vivid recollections of being cut from the vehicle, the noises and the excruciating, terrifying pain. When he was a small boy, like most children, he had an occasional nightmare but a warm milky drink and a cuddle wasn't going to cut it this time. These images stayed with him for years. Yet somewhere deep within he found the strength not only to carry on but was determined to recover in every way possible. I assume he took on board the advice from Sister Miranda, and indeed Olivia, because he asked to meet with the hospital Chaplain. He needed someone's blessing to put his grief aside for a while to concentrate on learning to walk again, and felt that the chaplain could offer him that. The wisdom and courage Aaron displayed was monumental and my admiration knew no bounds.

The first challenge was for Aaron to sit up in bed. Because he had spent the last three weeks or so laying on his back and was recuperating from major spinal surgery, this wasn't as easy as it sounds. What should have been a simple task was exhausting for him. When they finally got him into an upright position, the colour drained from him and he felt sick. I now know that this is partly due to a change in blood pressure caused by the loss of spinal fluid, as well as the shock to his body. However, after a few days Aaron was finally able to sit upright.

The Place Where Miracles Happen

The next step was to get him in a wheelchair. Heather was desperate to see Aaron, and he felt ready to see her, so we arranged for her to visit the spinal unit. Aaron was in a private room and, as Heather and I sat with him, the nurses came in wheeling the dreaded hoist that they would use to lift him into the wheelchair. As he lay in bed, the staff put him into what I could best describe as a kind of hammock, then the electric hoist was used to lift him. Frankly he looked like a carcass with his legs dangling lifeless and a look of sheer horror on his face, it was a pitiful sight. This was the first time I had seen it, Steve had tried to warn me that it wasn't pleasant to watch but nothing could have prepared me for what I was witnessing. I didn't understand why, considering he was completely paralysed from the waist down, this was such an excruciatingly painful experience for Aaron, but it was. He was screaming, begging them to stop. I had to fight the maternal urge to pull them away from him. At some point during the commotion Heather and I got trapped in the room, I wanted to spare her the agony of seeing this but there was nothing I could do to get her away. She turned to me, took my hand in hers and quietly said, "Now I understand why it was Jack that died, he would never have been strong enough to do this and I couldn't bear to see him try." Wow. Bizarrely this had given Heather a brief moment of clarity and possibly comfort. It gave me an opportunity to feel a little less self-indulgent, this whole experience really was as horrifying as I perceived it to be.

The weeks passed and we became more familiar with the way of life on the spinal unit. The rehabilitation process basically comprised of four main wards, from acute care through to a facility dedicated to preparing the patient for their final discharge and we would, over the coming months - though for some patients and families it would be years - progress through each of these stages. I'm not sure at what point we stopped being the newbies and came to see the unit as our second home - but we did.

It was in the very early days that Aaron would lay in bed and desperately try to move his toes. He could barely sit up to be able to see his feet so he would ask me to check for him. It was so tempting to pretend I had seen movement but he made me promise to

The Place Where Miracles Happen

always be honest with him. So day after day I would watch intently for the slightest flicker only to shake my head and tell him: "Not this time, but you will." Until one day... there it was! I screamed! There was movement. So slight you could barely see it, but it was definitely there. The look of exhilaration on his face was priceless. There was a feeling of excitement in the air, progress finally. The whole family were elated, for us this meant that a signal was getting through from the brain to the muscle, there was something to work with. If this was possible then anything was possible. To be honest I had lost all faith until that moment, when hope revealed itself in the tiniest of movements. I didn't care that Mr. Newton wasn't able to share our enthusiasm, I instinctively knew that this was the start of something big and no-one would convince me otherwise. This was the place where miracles happen. Cathy brought her video recorder to the unit and told Aaron to get everyone to record his progress from that day forward, because he was going to walk again and one day his story would inspire others.

F*ck the Biscuits

Every day since we had arrived, Aaron had been asking when he was going to see a physiotherapist. He was desperate to make a start on his recovery and learn to walk again. An entire team had been assigned to him consisting of a physiotherapist, an occupational therapist, and a psychiatrist, as well as the team of consultants headed by Mr. Newton. Mark and I were sitting with Aaron in his room when a young woman came in and introduced herself as the physiotherapist who would be working with Aaron. He looked so excited, at last it was time to get this show on the road. We left them to it and waited outside the room.

Then I heard a chilling scream, it was Aaron. He was enraged, shouting at the top of his voice and throwing things everywhere. Anything he could reach from his bed he was hurling across the room. I was terrified. I couldn't deal with it and ran out of the ward, down the corridor and found myself in a relative's room with my hands over my ears trying to block out the sound. It wasn't that I was scared of Aaron, I was scared of his pain. After Sister Miranda had given me the heads up about anger being one of the emotions Aaron would at times feel, I made a pact with myself that no matter how bad it got, I would take it and deal with it. Yet here I was failing miserably. I just couldn't bear to hear him like that. Mark eventually found me, I looked up at him and pleaded with him to take care of Aaron because I was of no use to him. After a while I made my way back to Aaron's room to find him in a bear hug with Mark, who had taken everything out of reach so he had nothing left to throw and was holding him tight until eventually he had calmed down. Before I had a chance to enquire as to what was going on and ask what had been said to trigger such a response, Mr. Newton appeared. He calmly told Aaron to listen to no-one but him, that he was in charge of his rehab and he made all the decisions. I later learnt that when Aaron had asked about starting his treatment, the physiotherapist had made it perfectly clear that he was there to be rehabilitated for life in a wheelchair, not to learn to walk. The only people that could help him had already given up on him. Can you imagine how that must have felt?

F*ck the Biscuits

By the time we left the unit that day, Aaron had calmed down and was sleeping. I phoned Steve to tell him what had happened and he told me that he also assumed the physio had got it all wrong. Later that evening Steve made the two-hour drive to the hospital and sat with Aaron through the night while he slept. Aaron woke to find his dad by his side. Thank God one of us was a strong and loving parent, because I certainly didn't feel like one. I hated myself and felt that I really had let my son down. Sadly though, I would be given ample opportunity to put that right. We had yet to face the biggest heartache.

CHAPTER SIX

The Funeral

I had been in fairly close contact with Heather since we first met after the accident so I was pretty much aware of all the funeral arrangements. The build-up to it was an intense roller coaster for all of us but for different reasons. Aaron was obviously very weak, in poor health and almost totally dependent on the hospital staff. Endless meetings took place with his medical team to determine whether or not he would be allowed to attend. Aaron was unaware of this and assumed that he would be going, he wouldn't entertain any other idea anyway. I felt caught in the middle: what if they refused? One day it would seem that he could go, only for the opinion to change again. Every waking hour it was all I could think about, Aaron would be completely distraught if he wasn't allowed to go. He couldn't miss it. By now the time seemed to be passing by quickly and I had another concern to add to an endless list of worries, what if they wouldn't facilitate him attending? But to her absolute credit, and as a testament to her strength, Heather postponed the funeral and made it clear that she would not go ahead until Aaron could be there.

The one saving grace was that Mr. Newton completely understood that Aaron should attend for the sake of his psychological well-being if nothing else. He was a fair man and didn't want to undermine his team, respecting their professional opinions. It was eventually decided that, if the physio team were in agreement, he should go. My relief was palpable when, a few days later, Mr. Newton came bearing good news. Aaron would be allowed to attend, knowing that the emotional and psychological benefits outweighed the risks. Up until now I had assumed that we would have at least one member of medical staff who would be coming with us, but this was not the case. I was horrified when Steve and I were asked to meet with the team to be given instructions for the day. The funeral was to be held some one hundred or so miles away, so suitable transport had to be organised. I didn't think

The Funeral

this would be a problem, Mark was a taxi driver with a wheelchair accessible vehicle. First problem solved, or so I thought.

Aaron was on a concoction of drugs so Steve and I had a crash course on how to administer them, as well as guidance on what to do should he lose consciousness or any other possible issues arise. We were shown how to empty his catheter and were also given emergency telephone numbers for differing medical centres en route in case we got into difficulty. I was terrified to say the very least, this was too much. The responsibility felt completely overwhelming. Thank goodness Steve seemed to be fairly calm and in control, though I suspect he was as scared as I was. I am grateful that he was able to show such strength, not just then but throughout this entire ordeal.

Then there was the bloody outfit that became the bane of my life. Understandably, Aaron wanted to look his best. Not just for himself but, more importantly, for Olivia and Jack. I took his suit to the hospital, somewhat inevitably it didn't fit. He was such a small and frail version of his former self. How on earth was I going to find the time and energy to go shopping for a new suit? I did though, and some shoes too (although we only actually needed one shoe because one of his feet was still in a cast). Neither the suit nor the shoes were right, Aaron wasn't happy with them. I took them back and tried again, this time the suit was okay but not the shoes. I felt incredibly guilty, the shoe fitted - did it really matter that he didn't like them? I was getting frustrated, did he have any idea how time consuming this was? Then I glanced across to where he sat in his wheelchair next to his bed and I saw the look on his face. It mattered a lot, that much was clear. How could I be so selfish? On the third attempt I got the shoes right. We were finally good to go.

Mark had mentioned at some point to me that he didn't think his vehicle would be suitable to take Aaron to the funeral, vaguely explaining why but in honesty I wasn't really taking much notice. There was enough going on, the vehicle would be fine - it's what it's designed for. I pretty much ignored the problem in the hope that it would go away, and I thought it had. It was decided that Steve would go with Mark to Stoke

The Funeral

Mandeville the night before so that Steve could be with Aaron first thing in the morning, to help him get ready. More importantly, of course, to be his emotional support. Mark would then have his vehicle already at the unit to take them to the funeral and back again. Off they went, it seemed quite bizarre to see both my ex-husband and soon-to-be new husband planning a night together in a hotel room. Nothing in our world was normal anymore, this was just one more thing.

I was to stay behind and go directly to the funeral with Cathy. The morning came, I could literally feel the grief in the air around me even though I was alone in the house. Nearly everyone I knew would be there, I had a tremendous number of messages of love and support. Heather and Aaron were all I could think about, I prayed that they would have the strength to make it through the day.

There was one final thing I needed to do to get ready to face this day, and that was to apply my special eyeliner. While we were in Amsterdam, Olivia had been putting on her make-up when Sue noticed that she had some pink glittery eyeliner. We all fell in love with it, this product certainly brought out the girlies in us. Sue took it upon herself to source this eyeliner and buy one for each of the women who came to the hen weekend, we were all to wear it on the day in memory of Olivia. There was something extremely bonding in seeing us all wearing our pink glittery eyeliner. It was a wonderful idea and I have no doubt that Olivia would have loved it.

Cathy came to collect me and I could tell instantly that something was wrong. It transpired that Mark had asked Steve if they could take his car to the hospital as he had booked a separate wheelchair accessible vehicle to go to the spinal unit to collect Aaron. He didn't want to drive himself, and the last time Cathy had spoken to Steve, the taxi still hadn't arrived. What the hell? It was a two-hour drive, they were unlikely to make it in time. I was furious with Mark, didn't we have enough to deal with without this? It also clearly hadn't occurred to him that Aaron was petrified to even get in a vehicle for obvious reasons, let alone to be on the M25 with a stranger at the wheel. Unbelievable! But

The Funeral

there was nothing I could do about it, except worry of course. I was getting good at that by now.

I am sure Mark had his reasons for doing what he did, although not one of us understood why he would do such a thing, yet nothing was said, there seemed little point. We had bigger fish to fry. Eventually we got the call to say they were on their way and all we could do was hope and pray that they would make it on time. They did, just as the hearse arrived.

The taxi pulled up as near as it could, but the road next to the church was utter chaos. Cars parked everywhere, onlookers watching as the coffin arrived in a horse-drawn hearse. The horses were more a tribute to Olivia who was a keen young horsewoman, her colleagues and friends from the stables where she kept her own horse were following the hearse wearing their riding outfits and hats. It was a spectacular sight. There was only one coffin, Heather wanted them to be buried together - side by side as brother and sister. She wanted Jack to take care of his little sister.

F*ck the Biscuits

It was crazy trying to get into the church, there were a few people pushing as they tried to keep with Heather and we had no choice but to do the same. They weren't being rude or unkind; they were simply standing by her side. I totally got it. Steve pushed the wheelchair through and I clung on tight! Aaron was extremely anxious about being in his wheelchair, not just because he would be seeing so many people for the first time since the accident, but also because he felt incredibly vulnerable. He was extremely weak and in poor health, but that wasn't the only reason.

Part of the rehabilitation process for wheelchair users is to become accustomed to being physically lower than those around you and to learn how to ensure people respect your personal space. Aaron was nowhere near that stage, he had hardly left the hospital ward and had quickly become institutionalised in this one safe environment. For this reason, he had begged a couple of his close friends to stay with him at all costs, and they did. Those young people had a job to do and they were absolutely determined not to let Aaron down. It was imperative we all sit together. I was also carrying a very large bottle of water and did get some strange looks, but Aaron was to drink plenty of fluids so he didn't pass out. No pressure then.

There were also a few plain-clothed police officers in attendance. This was to ensure journalists were not present and to keep them away. All the guests had been warned about a possible intrusion from the media and were asked to keep an eye out for anyone acting suspiciously or taking photographs. Fortunately, they stayed away and respected our privacy, but the possibility was one more thing to be concerned about.

We finally sat down near Heather and her family. I took a moment to take stock and look around. There were so many young people stricken with grief, accompanied by their parents who also looked confused and dazed. This was new territory for us all. There were beautiful flowers in the church and two large pictures, one of Olivia and one of Jack, both looking so young, carefree and happy. As I glanced at the coffin, which was wide enough for two, I felt such a raw sorrow and I could feel my heart pounding as I thought about how easily that could have been my son in there. I blocked this thought out before it could take hold, I had to keep focused to get Aaron through what was going to be one of the hardest days of his life.

I could see my family and friends all gathered in the church, so many appeared to look our way with concern which I later discovered was because they were completely shocked as to how ill and feeble Aaron appeared. Many of them had not actually been able to visit him yet, so seeing him like that was a lot for them to take in. When I look back on photographs of Aaron in hospital at the time, I can understand how they must have felt. My dearest friends were smiling at me, I could feel the love they were sending my way and despite everything else I also felt blessed that day. Blessed to have people in our lives that loved and cared for us so deeply, and simply that my son was alive. Guilty too, unbelievably guilty, but more about that later.

The service finally began. Music was played that you wouldn't necessarily expect to hear at a funeral but, of course, this was for two young people and the songs chosen reflected that. Many of Olivia's and Jack's friends made tributes to them and I was in awe of their courage and strength, even though they broke down and wept, they still kept going. Aaron had written a poem for Olivia, it was incredibly touching. He sat one night until the early hours writing it in hospital. When he showed it to me the next day, I tried to be brave but all I could do was weep, the tears falling down my cheeks. This poem was a reflection of his love for Olivia and his pain at losing her, it gave me a clearer insight into his inner thoughts and feelings and it absolutely broke my heart. The vicar read this poem on his behalf, and as he did so I could see the depth of Aaron's sorrow in his eyes. All I could do was hold him in the hope that I was able to give him some strength and comfort.

I can't speak of Heather's grief, how could I possibly begin to know how she must have felt? My older sister had died several years earlier and I will always remember my mother saying that there is no pain greater than outliving your children. That says it all.

After the service, we all made our way to the graveyard for the committal, even this wasn't an easy task. Poor

Steve was really struggling to push the wheelchair on the long grass, it seemed that everything we tried to do was just so bloody difficult. But nothing was as agonising as watching a mother bury two of her children.

The wake was held in a hall adjacent to the church, this was also beautifully decorated with a lot of thought and attention to detail. As the day went on, we all started to relax a little bit, I even managed to empty Aaron's catheter relatively painlessly for us both, go me! His anxiety about being amongst so many people slowly subsided and he was starting to feel more and more at ease. It was so good to see him chatting to all these amazing young people who had really pulled together to help and support each other, and to relatives and friends who had been so desperate to see him.

As I glanced around the hall, I noticed what I thought to be two large books, sitting on tables set in opposing corners of the room. One blue, the other pink. I went to investigate and was completely blown away. They were albums, filled with photographs portraying the lives of Olivia and Jack from babies through to their passing. Only one person could have poured so much detail and love into creating these, and when I later asked Heather how she could possibly have found the strength to do such a thing, she simply and quietly replied, "It was the only thing left that I could do for them". These powerful words portrayed the strength of a mother's love.

This may sound a little strange but the funeral was beautiful. It was harrowing, it was heartbreaking but it was nevertheless beautiful. Heather really had done them both proud. She did herself proud too, it goes without saying that she was extremely tearful but still she conducted herself with dignity and pride.

It was finally time to make our way back. Steve, Mark and I went in the taxi with Aaron who was by now absolutely exhausted. Steve administered Aaron's drugs and I got the picnic out. As well as plenty of fluids, it was important that Aaron try to eat, particularly as he was on a concoction of numerous tablets, so I had packed a good supply of food which everyone was grateful for, it had been a long and arduous day. There was still a bit of an elephant in the room concerning this taxi. It was a huge minibus with Aaron sitting up high in the middle in his wheelchair feeling terribly exposed and unsafe, Mark's vehicle would have been much more suitable and we all knew it. To make matters worse the driver was clearly in a hurry to get back, he put his foot down and I could see Aaron's anxiety level rising. He was taking deep breaths trying to keep himself calm. We were hoping Aaron would sleep and rest but at this rate that wasn't going to happen.

As the tension was mounting, the driver had to suddenly break sharply on the motorway. Aaron screamed. I can only begin to imagine what must have gone through his mind in that moment, the terrifying memories of the accident. Steve was absolutely livid, and it's fair to say he made that perfectly clear to the driver. What should have been a quiet time of reflection was yet another harrowing ordeal. I felt like screaming to the whole world to just leave Aaron alone, he'd had enough. It was my job to protect him and I was failing miserably. Suffice to say the

The Funeral

atmosphere between Mark and me that night wasn't exactly great.

We finally arrived back at the spinal unit, I'm tempted to say home because that's how it had begun to feel. We were all weary and Aaron settled into bed, we chatted for a while about the day, there was a sense of peace despite the heartache. Olivia and Jack were laid to rest and the day we had been dreading was now over. I checked in with Heather's friends, she was okay and sleeping. We did it, another challenge faced and accomplished. But it was far from the last.

F*ck the Biscuits

For what is it to die but to stand naked in the wind and to melt into the sun?

And when the earth shall claim your limbs, then shall you truly dance.

Kahlil Gibran

IN LOVING MEMORY OF TWO BEAUTIFUL SOULS

CHAPTER SEVEN

Life in the Spinal Unit

I don't entirely recall the days that followed the funeral with any clarity, but I clearly remember how our journey to recovery began. I made the four-hour round trip to the spinal unit every day, and on this particular day I had no sooner stepped onto the ward when Aaron said in a rather frenzied and urgent tone, "Mum, you need to get me the Bruce Lee video". I was clueless, but that was nothing new by now. I wasn't concerned that I had no idea what he meant, this was the first time I had seen a glimmer of light and hope in Aaron's eyes and that was all that mattered to me. Unbeknown to me, Cathy had been to see Aaron to explain how vital it was that he utilise the power of his mind if he were to make a recovery and walk again. She explained to him that Bruce Lee had broken his back and was told that he would never again be able to perform martial arts and was also unlikely to walk properly again. She wanted Aaron to watch his film and be inspired.

In truth, Bruce Lee didn't actually break his spine, he badly injured his back. Realising his situation would end his career in the movie business, he endeavoured to recover from his condition and rehabilitated himself to a point where he could again practise martial arts and ultimately he proved the doctors wrong. He very much used the power of his mind, his determination and strong will. But he also took a lot of drugs, and his back injury caused him to suffer in pain for the rest of his life. In honesty, his story wasn't the greatest out there, but Cathy is no fool. The movie was exactly that, a movie. And we all know the Hollywood version is going to be fluffy, powerful, hyped with hope and will most definitely have a happy ending. She also knew that, as a twenty-one year old man, this would be a story that Aaron would relate to and be inspired by. She firmly yet lovingly told Aaron to ignore any doubt, to keep focussed, to believe in himself and use visualisation techniques and the full capacity of his mind to make his recovery a reality.

The power of a mother's love is a phenomenal thing but I am under no illusion that I could not have taken Aaron to the point where he is today alone. Steve and Cathy played a huge part, I simply gave Aaron the love he needed to overcome the arduous demands this process would make on him. I couldn't mend him, though I would have sold my soul to the devil if it meant I could, but I was able to comfort him in his hour of need and to share the highs and lows that were abundant and extreme. One other factor was absolutely paramount to his success.... Hope. I was determined from the very beginning that I would not let him lose hope. My love for Aaron has always been unconditional and inexhaustible, and I trust he felt that in his many hours of need. I did all that I could to ease his burden, though this often felt very little. The crushing feeling of hopelessness was sometimes overwhelming.

The other thing I could do was to pray, and pray I did. Every night before getting into bed I would light a candle and say my prayers, to any deity prepared to listen. It didn't matter how tired I was or how inviting the bed seemed, it felt of paramount importance not to miss a single night of prayers. I would simply offer thanks for the progress we were making and ask that Aaron be given the strength to overcome the challenges he faced. I always asked that Heather be given the love and support she needed and I would end by saying, "Please let him walk again, in return I promise to give something back". I really didn't quite know what I meant by that, but it became apparent over the course of time.

I told my family and friends about Aaron's determination to heal himself and they were all totally supportive. By now Aaron had been moved to the next ward in the process, this was where his rehab was to begin in earnest. I am forever thankful that I was completely ignorant to the fact that their idea of rehab was most certainly not the same as mine!

As I sat one day with Aaron on his ward, I looked up to see the smiling face of my sister, Tracy, walking towards us holding a very long sheet of card. "This is for you, Aaron" she said, as she unravelled a banner that she had made using the famous quote from

Napoleon Hill. It read: 'What The Eye of Man Can See and Believe He Can Achieve'. Watching Tracy put the banner on the wall above his bed filled my heart with love for her, she believed in my son and it was obvious that she loved him dearly. She too believed that this was the way forward, she was on our side. For me that was huge and helped to eradicate some of the feeling of isolation and loneliness. This banner took its rightful place above his bed for the entire duration of his stay at the spinal unit. Whenever he moved beds, the banner came too. I wonder at times if it played a part in someone else's journey. Did anyone read it and feel inspired? We'll never know, but it undoubtedly fulfilled its role for us.

Mainly because he was still grieving, Aaron would more often than not prefer to have the curtains around his bed on the ward closed, shutting the world out and affording him the opportunity to face his emotions in private. I had just arrived for my visit one day and as I approached, I could hear the sound of soft and quiet sobs coming from behind the screen. I slowly pulled the curtain back enough for me to get to him, and there he lay. It was a pitiful sight that ripped my heart in two. He was listening to music through headphones and looked up at me as I sat next to him. The pain in his eyes and the tears streaming down his face told me everything I needed to know. This is what heartache looks like. I looked at him with a knowing smile and nothing was spoken between us. He passed me the headphones and immediately I recognised the song as one that was played at the funeral. We both cried, sobbing gently in each other's arms. This was unbelievably cruel. Aaron appeared to be soulless, weak and vulnerable and it felt like time stood still as the life force was slowly draining from him. All I could do was share his pain, to try and absorb it. If only I could take it away. Running through my head was the thought: "Lord have mercy on him, please let this suffering end."

By now Aaron was able to transfer himself from the bed to the wheelchair with relative ease and was having daily physio sessions. His assigned therapist was a young woman named Georgie, she was extremely pleasant with a kind and gentle manner. At

Life in the Spinal Unit

times I wondered if he would be better off with someone a bit bigger and tougher, but I could not have been more wrong. We developed a good relationship with Georgie, which was just as well because I was probably spending more time with her than most of my loved ones. Physiotherapy became the centre of Aaron's entire world.

Every patient has a timetable to adhere to which is adjusted on a weekly basis. This consists mostly of occupational therapy sessions, physiotherapy in the gym, wheelchair classes, weekly lessons in bladder and bowel management, and talks on various related subjects ranging from sexual dysfunction to housing rights. Then there was regular attendance with a psychiatrist. Okay, let's be honest here, if you're not familiar with spinal injury then this surely has to be a huge eye opener. It was for me, until this happened to us I was naive enough to think that being paralysed was simply a matter of limbs not working, and I feel I should apologise for my ignorance. Believe me when I say that the actual paralysis is the tip of the iceberg for many.

F*ck the Biscuits

It was in the fairly early days that Aaron was told he would have to learn to self-catheterise, something he was understandably dreading. He point blank refused to do it for a while until the nursing staff had to get firm and force the matter. I got it, and I knew they were right, but my maternal instinct kicked in and I just wanted to protect him like I had always tried to do. As I waited patiently outside the screen around his bed, listening to him calling out in discomfort and frustration, telling the nurses he couldn't do it, it was all I could do to stop myself running in and telling them to leave him alone. To pull them away and hold him in my arms. I took myself off for a while, knowing that any action on my part was not going to benefit anyone. Just like all the patients before him, he conquered his fear and ultimately was able to use a catheter himself with relative ease, which was just as well because he had to do this for a number of years.

For the sake of a little dignity at least, I won't go into details but suffice to say that I vividly recall Aaron having an incident with his bowel movement in the early days in the hospital. That for me wasn't the issue,

Life in the Spinal Unit

the thing that struck and upset me the most was that he had absolutely no idea it was happening. This was when I became aware of the severity and implications of the situation he was facing. Frankly I found the scene disturbing and it preyed on my mind for a long time. I can't tell you the number of times I wished it were me instead, and this was one of them. Just to put things in perspective, I've spoken to several patients who have told me that if they had to choose between the ability to walk or regaining their toilet control and sexual function they would take the latter. That's huge and gives an enormous insight into the complexity and struggles involved.

I found the wheelchair lessons quite interesting. Patients were taught how to control a wheelchair in given situations, for example how to mount high kerbs and what to do if they fell out of the chair. Surprisingly, the atmosphere was often light hearted and the classes could be good fun at times. The tutor posed the question one day: "Can anyone think of a reason as to what might cause you to fall out of your wheelchair?". With quick wit Aaron replied: "About six pints?". Everyone laughed, including the tutor. As visitors, we were often asked to attend and assist. An eye-opening class was taken one day covering the subject of personal boundaries. With the best of intentions, people will sometimes see a patient in a chair and, without even asking first, will rush to their aid and try to 'help' by grabbing the chair and pushing it. The lesson was how to deal with a situation like this. I have seen the result for myself of someone doing just that with pretty devastating consequences. I was at a fundraising event, one that I had organised for Spinal Research, and there was a guy there in a wheelchair. He was not a young man and was quite portly, not only did he have his visible disability but he also suffered considerably with arthritis in the joints in his shoulders, an all too common result of pushing yourself around in a chair for prolonged periods of time. As he was about to go up a ramp, some random bloke grabbed the chair and started pushing it hard. The chap tried to tell him to stop but it was too late. As he ascended the ramp at speed it forced his weight back causing the chair to tumble over backwards, he was unable to help himself because of the problem with his shoulders. It was a dangerous situation, the guy and his chair went flying. This is one of the important reasons why patients are taught to deal with personal boundaries.

Aaron loved his physio sessions, even though they were gruelling and physically exhausting, he couldn't get enough. For him this was the path to walking again and absolutely nothing was going to stand in his way. The staff would joke that the reason the gym was locked at night was to keep Aaron out so he could get some sleep. He would have been in that gym 24/7 if he had his way. It was of huge benefit that up until the accident Aaron had been physically fit because he was a very keen footballer. In fact, that was yet another issue for him to come to terms with. It took him a long while to adjust to the fact that he was never going to play football again, and he has never played since. Football was a huge part of his life, when he was only 6 years old he was head hunted by Colchester United and played in their junior league for several years. True, it wasn't exactly the Manchester United that he had dreamed of, but nevertheless it was an achievement and playing the game had always given him immense pleasure. This was just one more thing that had been ripped out from underneath him, and it bothered him for a long time.

The life that Aaron knew no longer existed. It was far from being just about the football. He was a qualified vehicle technician with Jaguar, and it was highly unlikely that he would ever be fit enough to be able to return to his career. Having been cut from the wreckage of a vehicle and remembering every single moment of it, I was never sure that he would want to work with cars again anyway. He told me that because he understood exactly how an engine works, he was able to tell that the vehicle was about to lose control before the others realised. He knew they would crash at 70 miles per hour. They do say ignorance is bliss.

Now his girlfriend and best friend were no longer at his side, dealing with this loss was a lonely path. It was years later that Aaron recalled some of this pain, he explained the intense loneliness and fear that he lived with every day. The feeling of being alone was with him every moment of every day. Trust me when I say that was not easy to hear. Aaron was no stranger to grief, with my mum's passing he sadly learned how painful bereavement can be, but at least then he had Olivia and Jack in his life to ease the heartache and help him through. Most of the youngsters in their circle of friends were experiencing grief for the first time in their lives, they pulled together and supported one another as I watched on with a sense of pride and admiration. I was proud to know these young adults and to have them in our lives. I knew a few of them really well, Aaron had grown up with them, and I felt blessed as I witnessed their devotion to my son, they were of great comfort to me too, each in their own special way. As were Aaron's extended family, technically step-brother and step-sisters, but in reality very much his siblings. They were amazing then and they're amazing now.

Since that eventful meeting with the physiotherapist not long after we first arrived, Mr Newton had never actually said whether Aaron would walk again or not. He did say, however, that for them to have anything to work with, there would need to be a defined muscle flicker in his leg. It must be a flicker that Aaron was able to generate himself, and not a spasm. Aaron was determined to make this happen, apart from anything else he had to make them believe in him. This was the toe movement scenario all over again, except this time he could see for himself, he was able to sit up unaided now. Day in, day out, he would try so hard, the sheer determination on his face was both heartening and disturbing. I wanted this so badly for him, but the mum in me also wanted to tell him not to worry, not to be so tough on himself. That familiar feeling of wanting to make this okay, to take all of this away and make it better. But I knew not to say anything, this wasn't about me and to stop trying so hard would make things easier for me, not Aaron.

A few times we saw something. The first time this happened we were excited. Our hopes were quickly dashed when Mr. Newton took a look for himself and said that it wasn't the flicker he was looking for, it wasn't enough. Nothing was going to stand in Aaron's way, he stuck with it until eventually we saw it, this appeared to be different somehow and we called again

Life in the Spinal Unit

for Mr. Newton. When he arrived, I could see that he had no expectations, as if he was just going through the motions. It was then that I realised he had set this challenge not really expecting it to be met, instead it would be a gradual way for him to introduce Aaron to the concept of rehabilitation for life in a wheelchair. I am overjoyed to report that his plan well and truly backfired. Our joy was as great as Mr. Newton's shock, this was indeed exactly the type of muscle flicker he was looking for. I could tell that things would change from then on. Something had just happened, I could feel it. This was the day that Mr. Newton began to view Aaron differently and was the beginning of his belief in him. I later learned that after this incident Mr. Newton approached his team and told them to keep a careful eye on Aaron, that there could just be something different about him, and to observe closely and see how things pan out.

By now I had a routine. I went to the hospital most days on my own as Mark was back at work, but I would have the odd day at home while others visited. I did have offers from people volunteering to take me there, and sometimes I took them up on their offer, but for the most part I drove there myself. As anyone would imagine, there were considerable lows. Every day brought another challenge, physical or physiological. I quickly learned to take each day as it came.

It soon became apparent to me that, whilst the unit was very well equipped, the food was not quite up to scratch. I felt it was important that Aaron have a well-balanced, nutritional diet and this was something that I provided for him. Every day I bought him a home-cooked meal, don't ask me how I had the time for this because I've no idea. All I do know is that this was one of the few things I could actually do to aid his recovery, so I was determined to make it happen. With every journey, the M25 seemed to get slightly longer, especially with a chicken stew and home-cooked vegetables precariously balanced on the front seat! I would often make enough meals to last for a few days and I recall going to the fridge on the ward one day where I knew I had left a meal, only to find it gone. To say I overreacted is an understatement. I was furious, that food was meant for Aaron, I had lovingly prepared it and now it was gone. Because I hadn't labelled and dated it correctly, the cleaning staff had thrown it out. When I learned this, I got upset and I cried. It wasn't enough that the food had gone, on top of that it was my fault. It seemed to matter so much which is crazy, I somehow doubt that it was a priority for Aaron.

I was so sensitive to everything. It wasn't about the food. My dear friend Jan and I have a saying... 'It's never about the bread'. That was born after we visited a farm shop one day having been enticed in by some very scrummy-looking loaves of bread. Jan is an amazing artist and produces the most beautiful greeting cards and prints, amongst other things. In the shop she started talking to the owner and by the time we left it had been agreed that they would have a stand with her cards and artwork to sell in their shop. What a lucrative visit that turned out to be. We didn't buy any bread, we were drawn to the shop for a reason but it 'wasn't about the bread'! Things are rarely about what you first think they are, and my mini breakdown was definitely not about a meal.

F*ck the Biscuits

"Hi mum, can you bring me a pilates belt tomorrow please? Sorry, you weren't asleep were you?" No, Aaron, it's almost 2 o'clock in the morning, why would I possibly be asleep? I wasn't annoyed at being woken at this unearthly hour, I was willing to do whatever I could to help and I felt grateful that he had called me. Apparently, Aaron had been in the gym earlier that day where they had used a pilates belt to hook around his feet so that he could pull on the belt in order to stretch the tendons and muscles in his feet and ankles, he could also use it to stretch his hamstrings. His toes were starting to contract and curl. In fact they are still curled to this day, and probably always will be to a degree. That night he had figured out a way to do this himself from his bed, he was frustrated when he lay on the ward doing nothing and felt it was precious time wasted when he could be making progress with his recovery. As he was dozing off, he had a sudden thought that I could get a belt for him and bring it in the morning. I intended to leave at around 8 o'clock the following morning, so this was a challenge to say the least. It was wonderful to have a network of friends willing to do whatever they could to help, so all I can

Life in the Spinal Unit

say is: "Thanks Jeanne, I owe you much love and a pilates belt!" This is just one small example of Aaron's determination and tenacity and the last thing I was going to do was stand in his way.

Weeks turned into months and the spinal unit had quickly become my new world, my life was centred around it with little room for anything else. Our greatest focus was the gym and Aaron's physio sessions. I did my utmost to be there most days, though I was usually at the mercy of the M25 if he had an early appointment, but I gave it my best shot. As a family we did a lot of filming with the video camera in the gym, capturing Aaron's journey. We did get permission to do this which was granted on the condition that no other patients were filmed or appeared in the footage.

Watching Aaron at work was not easy. It was often painful, arduous and exhausting for him. I would simply sit and observe, the pain and sheer willpower on his face was difficult to bear at times but I hope I never showed it. There were so many times when I wanted to tell him to stop, to rest. Enough now. But I

F*ck the Biscuits

never did, if he was going to walk again he would need every ounce of determination he could muster, so it was to be encouraged. The gym itself was amazing, with every piece of equipment imaginable and the staff were beyond incredible. Physiotherapy is designed to help with joint mobility, muscle strengthening and splinting, pain management, balance training and strengthening the gait, as well as posture and seating. In truth, Aaron wasn't interested in that, this was for people confined to a wheelchair and he was going to walk out of there if it killed him, and there were times when I thought it just might.

Pain management is an interesting one, I've never quite understood how you can have absolutely no feeling from below your point of injury and yet can experience such pain, as Aaron frequently did. Clearly something to do with the nervous system, but beyond that I'm no doctor. Watching from the sidelines as my child experienced acute agony from the simplest of movements was too much sometimes. I would occasionally feel overwhelmed and quite nauseous but I couldn't walk away, if Aaron could do this then I

Life in the Spinal Unit

certainly could. I never let him see what was really going on with me, I tried to only ever let him see my enthusiasm and encouragement. What I truly felt in that gym could wait until I was alone with my thoughts. One of my biggest regrets to this day though is that this wasn't always the case outside of the gym, there were times when I felt low, tired and my sense of hope was nowhere to be found. I did try to disguise how I felt, but there were times when I simply didn't try hard enough.

Aaron was a long way from walking. He had progressed from the muscle flicker to very simple movement. My friend Pip came to the unit one day to cut Aaron's hair for him. She came with me for the day so we were together in the gym watching Aaron have his physio session. He sat on the edge of a bench and was trying to lift his leg from the knee, and from the look on his face you would think he had an incredibly heavy weight attached to his foot. Just at the point where I was wishing Aaron would give up for the day it happened! His foot lifted by several inches, clearly visible and clearly significant. Pip and I were over the moon, we yelped in excitement but were soon put in our place. Georgie told us not to get over-enthusiastic, it was good but it didn't mean anything. It might not have meant anything to her, but it did to us, and if you could have seen the look on Aaron's face it was obvious that it meant everything to him. Some fifteen years later, Pip and I still talk of that day in the gym so it clearly left an impression on us. I understand that NHS staff have to be very careful about making promises that they can't guarantee to fulfil so I wasn't too concerned, and simply put all their caution down to this. Looking back, I realise now that I made a choice in that moment to be naive.

I've no idea who, but someone mentioned that any amount, or type, of stimulation to the legs helps to activate the nerves and signals in that area. The more varied the type of stimulation the better. This was why Aaron's bedside cabinet came to have a box on the top storing such things as tin foil, feathers, a metal comb, a hairbrush, cotton wool, a wooden back-scratcher, the list is endless. We had massage oil too, and he would regularly benefit from a foot and leg massage. All of his visitors were asked to do their bit and would be stroking Aaron's legs with any of these items as they sat and chatted with him. I don't know if it made any difference, all I do know is that anything was worth a try and I would often come across suitable bits and pieces and add them to the box. Maybe people thought we were a bit crazy, maybe we were, but if I'd have been told to do a handstand singing three verses of Hallelujah because it would help then I'd have done it! These were desperate times and they called for desperate measures.

Aaron's fight for his mobility didn't end in the gym. Cathy taught him how to use meditation and visualisation techniques. For example, he would lay in bed and begin by imagining the feel of the sheets under his legs, then move on to feeling the ground under his feet. He would then envisage the feel of grass underfoot as he mindfully walked, noticing every detail as he lifted each foot and placed it in front of him. He would take his mind to a place where he could walk and run, visualising it holographically, being aware of the emotions and sensations that he felt as he did this.

F*ck the Biscuits

He was unrelenting and I had nothing but admiration for his dedication. He once told me that if you were twenty-one years old facing the prospect of being wheelchair bound for the rest of your life you too would do anything. Fair point.

Visualisation works because when we use brain imagery, neurons in the brain (the electrically-charged cells that transmit information) interpret this imagery as equivalent to real-life action. When we visualise an act, the brain generates an impulse that tells our neurons to 'perform' the movement.

There have been endless studies and research which show this to be a proven technique. That may be so but not everyone has the courage and conviction to see it through. I say that with absolutely no judgement, I don't know if I could have done it. Although it made me super proud to see him take this on board, the flip side is that it's hard for a mother to hear and watch her child so desperate and so scared for the future. Visitors quickly got used to having to make themselves either scarce or useful, there's no way Aaron was going to waste time making small talk. Nothing was going to

Life in the Spinal Unit

stand in the way of him walking, and he knew he had to keep his mind focussed on exactly that. Aaron has never been someone to do anything by halves, and he would take this to a whole new level by imagining himself playing football - finally he was playing for Manchester United and winning!

Here's the extraordinary thing, as I watched him once lay in bed doing this I was astounded as he started to sweat and get out of breath, as if he literally was running and exerting himself for real. I have since learned so much about how the body responds to the mind that it is of no surprise to me now, but it was back then. My emotions were conflicted, on the one hand I truly believed in Aaron and I believed he would walk. But on the other hand, I had serious concerns that he was putting himself through all of this for nothing. I couldn't bear the thought of him putting all this effort in, only to fail. Failure haunted and scared me, I had no idea how I would deal with Aaron's emotions and get him through if he didn't succeed.

And there you have it – guilt. I still feel guilty to this day because in truth I was scared about how I would deal with his emotions, not just about how he would deal with them. The whole thing scared me so much, there were days when I just wanted to say enough is enough, just accept being in a wheelchair - do your rehab and make the most of it. Plenty of people go on to live perfectly happy lives with paralysis, you can too. Did I really mean that? No. Absolutely not. It was my fear taking over. I pray that I am right in believing I hid these thoughts from everyone, particularly Aaron. I successfully hid the way I felt because I was ashamed. Ashamed of my fears, ashamed of my thoughts. It was only the odd day here and there when I would feel like this, for the majority of the time I knew in my heart that he could, and would, walk again. The only thing that bothered me and gave rise to any doubt was the fact that not one single medical professional had ever actually confirmed this.

Let's talk about guilt. As a mum there are endless times when you feel emotionally torn and guilty, whether it's justified or not, we all know the feeling. It seems to be a fundamental part of parenting, we question ourselves and feel an element of guilt a lot of

Life in the Spinal Unit

the time. Over the years, I've often joked with other mums that I gave birth to a healthy baby boy and a bucket load of guilt and worry. Yet nothing prepared me for a condition referred to as survivor's guilt, or survivor's syndrome as it's also known. Aaron suffered with this big time and it ate away at him, I knew there was nothing I could say or do to stop it or make it disappear. The reason I knew this was because I was suffering too.

Survivor's guilt can occur in relation to a traumatic event or a loss of life. When a person survives an event that others did not, it can lead to feelings of guilt and they may question why they escaped death while others lost their lives. This was most definitely the case for us. Aaron described it as "feeling guilty just for being alive". It is very common, in fact in one survey it was found that over 90% of participants who had survived an event when others had died reported experiencing feelings of guilt. In truth, that was little consolation, although it did mean that the hospital was aware of it and treatment was available. I'm not sure how much the treatment helped Aaron even though he had a dedicated psychiatrist working with him. However, I do think that his greatest healer was time, and I hope the love I gave him also played its part. He had been thrown into a frightening world which was completely alien and needed time to heal, time to process and time to grieve. I would sometimes sit with Aaron and we would cry together whenever his grief and fears would surface.

Life was an emotional roller coaster. Survivor's guilt is also a significant symptom of PTSD - Post Traumatic Stress Disorder. Other symptoms of PTSD include flashbacks of the traumatic event, feelings of helplessness and disconnection, fear and confusion, and suicidal thoughts. Aaron later confessed that he too had suicidal thoughts at times. As with PTSD, survivor's guilt can cause a person to see the world as an unfair and unsafe place. It hurt me to the very core to know that Aaron was suffering with each and every one of these symptoms, and every day I tried to make his world feel a little safer. It was gruelling at times and I often asked myself how I could find it all so hard when at least my son was alive? I constantly felt torn,

Life in the Spinal Unit

my emotions pulling me in every direction. I too suffered a degree of PTSD, and did for many years, but the overwhelming thing for me was the guilt I carried every single day for a long, long time because my son had lived and Heather had lost two of her children. I felt guilty simply because my son was alive.

There were endless nights over a long period of time when Aaron would wake from horrific nightmares, reliving details of the crash and remembering vividly what it felt like to be trapped in the wreckage of the vehicle knowing the dark stillness of death was with him. As with most nightmares, his trauma was exaggerated in his dreams with frightening, horrifying scenes and images, all of which would haunt him the following day. I was always relieved in a strange way to take a phone call from him in the early hours of the morning to calm him down and soothe his mind. At least I was being of some use and it was good to know that he was willing and able to turn to me for help. There were times when it was exhausting for us both, it was yet one more thing to deal with and get through. But we did. Not once did Aaron let this take away his focus on his recovery, he battled through with such courage and I am as proud of him today as I was then.

Unbeknown to Aaron, both at the time and possibly up until now, his guilt led to another issue. Olivia and Jack's father, Michael, somehow got to hear that Aaron was feeling guilty. He was an angry man and didn't understand where Aaron's guilt stemmed from, all he saw was that if Aaron felt guilty then he had something to feel guilty about. He blamed Aaron for the accident, he was absolutely convinced that Aaron pulled on the handbrake which ultimately caused the crash. I suspect that the immense pain he felt for his loss ate away at him and gave rise to anger with the world and with Aaron. I was at home one day when the phone rang, it was Linda. Linda was the landlady of our local pub, she knew Mark and me well and Aaron, Olivia and Jack had spent a lot of evenings in her pub. She was devastated when she heard the news and was incredibly supportive, offering to do anything she could to help and cooking us free meals any time of the day or night. For the most part the only time I ate a decent meal throughout this entire ordeal was when I was tucked quietly away in Linda's restaurant, she was more than happy for us to just eat and go, I really didn't feel like socialising. She was a good friend and part of an amazing support network.

Linda had called to warn me that Michael had been to the pub, drank far too much and was on his way to my house to find Aaron. I won't repeat why he wanted to find Aaron, suffice to say it wasn't to chat with him. Linda had tried to stop him, she managed to get his car keys from him, but unfortunately we lived within walking distance. She suggested that as I was on my own, it would be a good idea to get out of the house. I took her advice without hesitation. My neighbours heard Michael banging on my door not long after that, so I was relieved to have done the right thing. This was just too much, not only was my home my sanctuary which had now been violated, but I had things to do, I didn't have time for this nonsense.

As far as my own emotions were concerned that was just the tip of the iceberg. I was scared. What if he went to the spinal unit? What if he found me and took his anger out on me? What if Aaron got to hear that he was being blamed for Olivia and Jack's death? He was barely coping with the myriad of thoughts, feelings and demons dominating his mind, this could tip him over the edge. I was furious. How dare Michael treat my son this way? Didn't he know what Aaron was coping with on a daily basis? Did he have no compassion or empathy? Part of me wanted to face Michael and have it out with him. I felt incredibly defensive of Aaron, but I knew I wouldn't be able to reason with this man. Not knowing how to handle the situation, I called Mark, he said he would get home as soon as he could and take care of it. I then phoned Steve, apart from anything else he had a right to know what was going on, this concerned Aaron's mental and physical safety. Steve told me to leave it with him and in the meantime if Michael found me and wanted to talk to Aaron, I was to dial Steve's number under the pretence that I was calling Aaron. The code for me needing help was for me to say to Steve something along the lines of "Hi Aaron, Michael is here and wants to see you". Steve would then come immediately, and I had every faith that he would. But I also knew that it wouldn't end well.

Life in the Spinal Unit

I didn't hear from Michael again and later learned that both Mark and Steve had been to his house to talk to him and make it clear that he was to leave Aaron and me alone. Whatever they said worked and I am so grateful for that. My stress levels had gone through the roof, but life went on and I would visit Aaron and give him all the love, encouragement and support that I could whilst hiding what was going on at home. That's what we do isn't it? Protect our young at whatever cost.

We got to know many people at the spinal unit, everyone was in there for the long haul and were going through the same system. Although, of course, for each one the journey is different. There was one young man, a few years older than Aaron who made himself known to us early on. Aaron had only been out of the acute ward for a few days when this lad came up to him and introduced himself as Eddy. He told Aaron how hard it was in the first few weeks but that it would get better and that if he needed anything at all just to ask. I guess because he'd been in the same boat, he would have known how much that small act of kindness meant to Aaron – and to me. It was comforting to know that there was someone on the 'inside' who had Aaron's back.

Eddy and Aaron became good friends, they were a similar age and ended up having some fun times together. I remember feeling pretty low one day, Aaron had gone to one of his classes and I was just having a bad day. Bad days were simply par for the course. I was alone so I could let my guard down and was shedding a few tears on the edge of the bed when Eddy appeared. He wheeled himself up to me, simply smiled and said "Coffee?". That's all he said but it was exactly what I needed, we went for a coffee and ended up having a giggle. Eddy must have had the world on his shoulders at times yet here he was cheering me up. His spinal cord was severed in a motorbike accident so he really was at the unit to rehabilitate himself for life in a wheelchair and, certainly from the outside looking in, he seemed to be doing well. His humour no doubt helped him through, and he often made me laugh. I do know though that at times he went to some pretty dark places, but would always bounce back to face another day.

The rehabilitation process is well thought through, and part of it is to get out and about so patients were encouraged to do such things as take a taxi into Aylesbury, which is the local town, do some shopping or go for a drink or meal as a means of adjusting to the 'real world'. We did just that, on a regular basis. I have pretty fond memories of being in the pub with Aaron, Eddy and some of the other youngsters, watching the football and experiencing an element of normality. Friends would often visit and take Aaron to the local pub, it's these simple pleasures in life that made everything bearable.

For the most part it all worked well, most venues were accustomed to accommodating wheelchair users, they were after all situated near to one of the biggest spinal injury units in the country. We were able to let our hair down a bit and temporarily forget what had now become our world, it was the same for all of us. There were always a few challenges along the way, such as the time Aaron's catheter needed to be emptied. The theory is that the catheter has a long enough pipe to be able to hook over a urinal or toilet seat but for whatever reason Aaron was wearing the wrong type so it wouldn't reach to be emptied into anything... except an empty beer bottle. Well, needs must! We laughed about that for days. I think that was the time when someone said "Aaron, I love your mum she's so bloody funny!" There comes a point when a sense of humour can feel like the only thing you have left.

I went to the shopping mall with several of this group of friends one day, I was supposed to be keeping an eye on everyone in case of any problems. No pressure then, there were about five of them, all young and full of beans. As soon as we got in there, they all whizzed off in their wheelchairs, it took me ages to catch up and find them. Puffing and panting I told them to slow down because some of us have no choice but to walk. I was familiar enough with them all by now to know that the joke would be taken in good faith and it was.

We would sometimes get a takeaway delivered to the ward, along with the odd beer or two which I'm sure was technically not allowed but nothing was said. It felt so good to see Aaron socialising and relaxing, it was a rare and beautiful thing. Each day over the next three months brought a mixture of progress, joy, disappointment, heartache and fun. Even in the face of such adversity we still managed some laughs.

I also made friends with some of the patients and their loved ones. There are so many heartbreaking stories but one woman stands out for me and is often in my thoughts. I sometimes wonder what became of her and her beautiful family. She was married with a young boy, I'd hazard a guess that he was about three years old. He was the cutest little man with stunning blonde hair and really reminded me of Aaron at that age. I think that's what drew me to them as a family – that and the fact that her despair and agony were about being a mum.

She had been on holiday with her husband and son in France when a vehicle freewheeled down a hill towards them. Because the engine wasn't running, they didn't hear it in time. Her husband was only able to save their son, she was hit by the car and it broke her spine. She was treated in hospital in France then flown to Stoke Mandeville for her rehabilitation. I don't know the extent of her injuries, but she was definitely being prepared for life in a wheelchair. Her little boy referred to the wheelchair as mummy's pushchair and she would often take him for a ride on her lap which was also a good way to familiarise him with the chair.

I remember sitting in Aaron's room one day when I saw the dear little boy ride past in the wheelchair on his own and we smiled but I was a bit concerned as to where mummy was, so I went to check to make sure she was okay and not stranded somewhere. On the odd occasion a patient would fall out of their chair unable to get back in, this was difficult to witness but it's how it was, everyone in the unit was on a huge learning curve in every way.

I would often chat with this woman in the ward, the kitchen or around the unit. She would talk to me about her heartbreak because she didn't know how to parent her son anymore, she felt she couldn't keep him safe and as a mum that's our purpose. She had lost her way and was no longer the mum she used to be. I couldn't begin to imagine how that must feel. Yet in a strange way I could relate, I hadn't changed but my son's needs had, and I wasn't prepared for this aspect of being a

Life in the Spinal Unit

mum. I was trying so hard to be the mum he needed me to be but at times I was grappling in the dark trying to figure out how to be the best mum I could to him. As much as I wanted to, I couldn't take this away from him, I couldn't make it better, and I couldn't fix him. All I could do was love him and hope that would be enough.

We met some remarkable people, all of us bonded by one thing: spinal injury. Each had a unique story, yet we all shared the same empathy, whether it be with other patients or their relatives and friends. From time to time, we laughed together, cried together and understood the anger and emotions that would inevitably emanate in us all at times. The ward kitchen was often where we would meet, chat and share our highs and lows, affording comfort and advice for us all.

There was a place in the unit where I would spend a lot of my time and that was in the cafe which, back then, was called Jimmy's. It was a good meeting place and somewhere to take myself away when I was feeling overwhelmed and didn't want Aaron to see. And somewhere to sit when Aaron was off the ward and I

F*ck the Biscuits

couldn't find him. The cafe was named after Jimmy Saville who had raised in the region of £40 million to fund the unit, and in the days when Aaron was a patient there, they still celebrated his involvement with the hospital. There were large pictures up on the walls at the entrance of him with Princess Diana when the unit was first opened. Apparently he was also supported in his fundraising by the then Prime Minister, Margaret Thatcher, whom he persuaded to donate £1 million of government money to the cause. We met the man himself in Jimmy's one day and he was just how I imagined him to be, wearing a shell suit and dripping in gold chains. It was four years later, a year after he died, that Jimmy Saville was exposed for his reign of sexual abuse at Stoke Mandeville since the 1970's, using his power and influence to gain access in the hospital where he was alleged to have sexually abused over 60 patients, visitors, staff and fundraisers many of whom were minors. Watching the news unfold on the TV, I was sickened to think we met him, shook his hand and thanked him for all he had done for the unit. The cafe has since been renamed and all reference to him has been removed from the hospital.

Life in the Spinal Unit

Aaron phoned me one evening, I hadn't been to the hospital that day. Steve and Cathy were visiting so I had the day at home. Aaron was so unbelievably excited, he'd been exploring around the hospital and grounds with his dad and they stumbled upon what we now know to be the Stoke Mandeville Stadium. The stadium was founded in 1948 by Ludwig Guttman. He was a neurosurgeon at the spinal unit who recognised the value of exercise and competition for wounded veterans and continued to expand the concept of organising sport for men, women and children with disabilities, ultimately developing the stadium into an international centre for disabled sport, leading to the Paralympic Games that we know today. The stadium is widely acknowledged as the birthplace of the Paralympic movement. They also have a large hydrotherapy swimming pool there, fully equipped with hoists, and Aaron had been told that he could have hydrotherapy too and the use of the pool whenever he wanted. This was huge for Aaron and he went on to enjoy hours in the hydrotherapy pool. This wasn't simply about another tool to aid his recovery, he told me that being in the water was the closest he got to feeling normal again. In water he was weightless, the inability to stand was insignificant and, with full use of his upper body, he was able to move freely in the water. This must have allowed him such an incredible sense of freedom. I often would accompany him to the pool, it was always a pleasure to watch him swim but to get in the water there was the dreaded hoist. I hated seeing him in a hoist, the vision of which I still find disturbing to this day.

Life was a roller coaster of exhausting highs and lows over the coming months. The highs were seeing improvements, often daily. What started with a tiny flicker of movement in a single toe, progressed to the ability to lift his feet, to tense leg muscles and complete numerous physical exercises in the physio gym. Every day it felt as if we were moving closer to the day when he would finally walk again. As difficult as it was at times, on the whole I was able to deal with the physical and medical issues involved because these could be left to what was an amazing team of specialists. It was the emotional and psychological trauma that was the hardest to watch. But my admiration for Aaron's

Life in the Spinal Unit

strength and determination will never leave me and I don't think any of us will ever truly understand how arduous the entire ordeal was for him.

I did my utmost to conceal it from Aaron, I needed to be his rock and I was determined to be just that, but I didn't have his strength. For the most part I felt broken and alone. I sat in my kitchen one evening, in a complete daze, wistfully staring into space, when Sue walked through the door. I looked up at her through teary eyes and quietly whispered, "I wish he would walk through that door... I wish he would walk." Then I broke down, I lay my head in my hands and wanted to shut the world out. I wanted a break, just for a day, from the constant anguish and despair that I felt every moment of every waking hour. I could cope with everything else, but I wasn't coping well with the fact that my son, who I had protected and kept safe all his life up until now, was broken and there was nothing I could do to change that, to mend him or give him any respite. The feeling of helplessness was the hardest to bear. I wanted Aaron to have my legs, my mobility.

I felt Sue's arms embrace me and felt her love healing me. I realised then the power of such love and knew that it was the gift of unconditional love that I could give Aaron. Love would find a way.

Not knowing what the future would hold I found to be incredibly tough. The burning question for me was "Will Aaron ever walk again?". This was a complete contradiction really, since I also believed that he would, I think this was more a case of not daring to believe otherwise. The alternative wasn't something I was ready to face. It got to a point where not knowing seemed harder than knowing for me. I even had a momentary yet shocking thought on the long drive home once that at least Heather knew the outcome, she knew what she was dealing with. What a hideous and cruel thought – but it shows how desperate I felt. I longed for certainty.

Not long after this I was having a coffee at Sue's house and a friend of ours was there, Debbie. We were talking about the whole situation, I was amongst friends and could let off a bit of steam. I confessed to this abhorrent thought. They totally got it and

Life in the Spinal Unit

reassured me that it was understandable. Then Debbie turned to me and gently said, "He will walk again." It was as if she knew something that we didn't. Whether that was the case or not, the fact remains that her words stuck with me and played over and over again in my head just when I needed to hear them. She is probably unaware of the impact she had on me that day, and I never thanked her, but I remain forever grateful.

After a few months I returned to work, initially for just one day a week. My first day back inevitably felt a little strange, and most of it was spent answering all the questions and responding to all the good wishes that came from colleagues and customers at the Post Office where I had worked for several years. I loved working in the heart of the community, it always gave me a sense of belonging and it felt good to be a part of something. Situated in an affluent area, the village is home to some real characters, including the wealthy widows who shop locally everyday with their wicker shopping baskets. One of them had a tiny dog which she would carry in her basket, they were devoted to one another. It is a diverse community, from the extremely well-to-do to those on low incomes. There are exceptions to the rule of course, but for the most part the one thing they have in common is that they are all very pleasant and interesting. The older folks, no matter what their background, have engaging tales to tell of life in their younger days. Sadly, though, so many are lonely. I have encountered too many women who have raised their children, supported their husbands and led full lives only to find themselves completely alone. Usually widowed, often their children have moved far away, some abroad, so family time is limited to high days and holidays at best. And they are denied the joy of watching their grandchildren grow up. Too old to travel on their own, they are at the mercy of their family to visit them. I would often think to myself how that must be so difficult. Ironically, I now find myself facing exactly the same possibility in years to come. I guess that's the price to be paid for raising independent and confident children who choose to live the life of their dreams. In honesty, I am proud of myself for that and unbelievably proud of Aaron and Amy for following their dreams.

It was wonderful to know that so many people really cared about us, they were such a support and my spirits felt lifted. I was smiling and chatting away, the normality of which was a breath of fresh air. Then at midday I received a telephone call from Mr. Newton who told me that Aaron had taken a fall from his wheelchair resulting in a possible twist in the scrotum, so he had been taken to theatre for a minor operation to correct it. However, when he was given the anaesthetic his heart immediately went into cardiac arrest and he crashed. The team of amazing individuals in the theatre had brought him back from the brink of death and he was now on a ventilator. Mr. Newton suggested that Aaron might need me and asked if I could make my way to the hospital as soon as was feasible. Yet again, one phone call had changed everything. One minute I was laughing and joking, the next I was shaking and panicking. Those around me took control, Mark was contacted immediately and a colleague took me home. I was in no fit state to drive. Before I knew it, we were in the car heading to the spinal unit which seemed a million miles away.

F*ck the Biscuits

We arrived to that familiar feeling that something pretty serious was going on. Escorted swiftly to the recovery unit in the theatres, I was quickly introduced as Aaron's mum and taken to the Sister in charge who explained that the anaesthetist hadn't realised that Aaron's spinal injury was less than six months prior so he gave him the wrong drugs. As soon as Aaron's heart rate rocketed prior to failure, he knew what had happened and immediately administered an antidote whilst the crash team revived him. Wow, such honesty was strangely refreshing. They were taking responsibility, I couldn't believe it.

When I saw Aaron lying still and lifeless on the bed, my first thought was that this was what I expected to see after his spinal surgery. He was so pale, he looked almost translucent. As I gently stroked his forehead, he came to a little, looked at me through dull and dreary eyes and simply gave a slight smile in recognition of my presence, then drifted back to sleep. By now they had taken him off the ventilator and after a good rest he seemed to recover fairly well considering. He was moved onto a ward by mid-evening, exhausted, and although his heart rate was not quite back to normal, he was definitely improving.

It was explained that they would need to keep an eye on him for a few days to ensure that no long-term damage had been sustained to the heart. My immediate thought was "You have to be joking, on top of everything else now you're telling me he may have heart damage." I looked upwards and said out loud, to who knows what deity, "Please just give us a bloody break!" It was much later that evening, in fact I had dozed off in the chair, when the anaesthetist appeared with Mr. Newton. He took a seat next to me and explained what had happened in the theatre and how sorry he was. He looked absolutely dreadful, there's me thinking I'd had a bad day, his was clearly worse. He came dangerously close to losing a young patient on the table. Despite everything, I not only felt such sympathy for him, but I also totally respected his frankness. Doubtless if the outcome had been different, I'd have felt very different, but I simply reminded him that his quick response had saved Aaron's life and advised him to put the day behind him, go home, have a stiff drink and a good night's sleep. He didn't respond with words, his response was far more powerful. He reached out, took both my hands in his and wistfully smiled with gratitude in his eyes. Not long after that Mark and I made our way home. I had a feeling that tomorrow was going to be a long one. I was right.

I left for the hospital early the next day. I was anxious to be with Aaron and to talk to the medical team to see how his heart rate was doing. I was tired, and so was Aaron. I spent most of the day in quiet contemplation while Aaron rested. It appeared that his heart, as far as they could ascertain, hadn't sustained any permanent damage and once he was strong enough, he could return to his rehab ward. This was obviously good news, but I was left feeling utterly useless and absolutely exhausted. I had no more energy, no more fight and it felt like I had nothing more to give. The shock was starting to emerge and I had lost control, facing your child's mortality once is traumatic, twice was just too much. I couldn't hide it from Aaron and even to this day I am so disappointed in myself for

Life in the Spinal Unit

letting my weakness control me, for letting him down and not being strong when he needed me.

It was a long but uneventful day and I started to make my way home mid-evening. I had a long drive ahead and felt physically, mentally and emotionally drained. I sat in my car and as I went to turn on the ignition, I fell back into my seat and screamed out loud, "That's it, I can't do this anymore!". I was hysterical, sobbing, punching the steering wheel and yelling for what seemed like an eternity. Eventually I ran out of steam, I didn't know how I was going to get home, I couldn't face the long drive. I slowly drifted back to an element of normality and reasoning, reminding myself that I had little choice in the matter. I decided to drive and if it all got too much I could pull over and find somewhere to stay and rest for the night. I made it home, having managed to make it through the lowest point in this living nightmare.

The last thing I want to do is to turn this into some kind of pity party, but I do want to honour my deepest fears and emotions throughout this journey in the hope that you can relate and find comfort in knowing you're not alone if you are going through a similar experience. And it wasn't all bad: as I mentioned, we met a lot of new friends in the unit with whom we shared not only our lows but also our wins, the good days as well as the bad. We were a community, often laughing and having a giggle, it was not just our experience but also our sense of humour that sometimes held us together.

A huge win took place in the gym one morning. One of the incredible pieces of equipment they had was an electric cycling machine that is designed to assist the rehabilitation of those with mobility challenges by using movement therapy. It is mainly used to improve circulation and is basically a motorised exercise bike for wheelchair users, you wheel up to the bike and strap your feet into the pedals whilst remaining in the wheelchair. The electronic bike will also measure any input from you showing on a digital counter as a percentage. Aaron used the bike a lot and the most he had managed on the scale was in the region of 0.02%, meaning the bike was only being powered by this with his own legs, but at least it was something.

Aaron had explained to me how he used his visualisation techniques on the bike. He would imagine cycling in the Tour de France: racing through the mountains, pushing on up to the front with the crowds cheering as they made their way down the Champs-Elysees to the finish line. All the time pedalling as hard as possible, feeling every emotion, every touch and how his body would be reacting to the strain. The pressure around him as the finish closed in. It wasn't until many years later I learned that he was motivated not only to strengthen his legs but he also used the opportunity to give his mind what he called a 'half an hour holiday' from the nightmare of his existence. Hearing this was powerful. He wanted me to accompany him whilst he did just that, and to look out for any increase in the percentage. Of course I was more than happy to help, but I wasn't expecting miracles, we had been here before remember. He wheeled up and strapped his feet in, switched the machine on and away he went... Before long he was in a trance, completely in a world of his own. Sweat was dripping from his face which was crumpled with determination, his breath quickened as he pushed harder and harder. I felt like an outsider looking in. I kept an eye on the counter, still only 0.02%. Just as I reached that familiar feeling of wishing he wouldn't be so hard on himself, something happened. Right in front of my eyes the counter slowly started moving, up and up it went until it reached an incredible 35%. Aaron's legs were powering the bike in a way that technically wasn't possible, but I was witnessing it with my own eyes. I started to shake and scream out to him. I needed Aaron to see this, I needed everyone to see this. I began shouting for attention. "He's doing it, look!" Aaron was jolted out of his meditative state by the commotion. Once he realised what had happened, we looked at each other with sheer delight, he threw his arms in the air in celebration. To me it didn't only feel like he had actually won the Tour de France, it felt like we'd won the lottery too! This was proof that the technique worked, and that his legs were capable of so much more than I had dared to dream. The mind is powerful beyond anything I understood at that time. I thought about Tracy's banner... "What the eye of man can see and believe he can achieve."

This seemed to be a turning point and Aaron made good progress from this time on. Interestingly, patients are given electrical stimulation as part of their treatment which can help facilitate and improve limb mobility along with other body functions lost due to injury such as respiratory, sexual function, bladder and bowel functions. When Aaron was resuscitated in theatre he was given a pretty hefty dose of electrical impulses several times and we sometimes wondered if it was not coincidence that his progress seemed to increase considerably following this. Mr. Newton would joke with us saying there may be some truth in it but he didn't think the anaesthetist would cope very well with any trials that might prove the theory! Fair comment. Whatever the reason, things were finally looking up.

Weeks had turned into months, with Aaron continuing to make steady progress. As part of their rehabilitation, patients are, over time, encouraged to go home at weekends if at all possible, to adjust to life outside the hospital environment. For the average home to accommodate a wheelchair user is not easy, but fortunately Steve's house did at least have a downstairs bathroom so Aaron, with a lot of help, was able to stay there some weekends. Although the bathroom was on the ground floor, the doorway was not wide enough for Aaron to get his wheelchair through so Steve would have to carry him to the toilet and the shower. I would invariably pay him a visit while he was at Steve and Cathy's and to watch Steve lifting Aaron and assisting him in every way possible, attending to his every need, did my heart good. Steve hadn't always been able to be there for either of us over the years but he was certainly making up for it now. The past no longer mattered.

Being local for the weekend also presented an opportunity for several of Aaron's friends to see him. Stoke Mandeville was too far away for many of them to visit, and it felt right to see him sitting on the sofa laughing and chatting with his mates. It was also a lovely time when his brother and sisters could be with him in a home environment and do what siblings do, teasing each other, giggling, ordering a takeaway, watching movies and playing games. These young adults were being afforded some element of normality amongst this craziness. The time always flew by, and home visits seemed to be over so quickly. Although Aaron was reluctant to leave, he was also eager to get on with his physio. His determination to walk again, and his belief that he would, never left him. Both served him extremely well.

FALLING

If we only knew then what we know now.

That love conquers everything.

That faith can move mountains.

That good things can happen to bad people and bad things happen to good people.

That loud doesn't mean strong and quiet doesn't mean weak.

That closed hearts are often hurt hearts that have yet to unfold.

That silence can be both beautiful and terrifying.

That healing takes time and time moves both quickly and unbearably slowly.

F*ck the Biscuits

That one step in any direction can change the course of your life forever.

That bliss is sometimes loving what you already have, rather than wanting what you wish you had.

That you will have days when you feel on top of the world and days where you feel like you have reached rock bottom.

And that rising from the ashes requires going through the flames.

And that falling was part of it all.

Ullie-Kay

CHAPTER EIGHT

F*ck The Biscuits

It was 1st December 2008, a date that will be etched on my mind forever. Christmas was fast approaching, and I had been helping Aaron to buy gifts for his friends and family. Wandering around the supermarket, I saw a tin of shortbread biscuits which I thought would make an ideal present for his Grandad, so I gave Aaron a call to see if he wanted me to buy it. No answer. This was nothing new – often he was in physio or busy and would call me back. I finished my shopping, then joined the queue at the petrol station, as I intended to leave early the next morning for the hospital. As I sat waiting in my car, my phone rang. It was Aaron and I assumed he was returning my call. I answered, thanked him for calling me back and instantly began babbling about the tin of shortbread biscuits, until I was abruptly interrupted. Aaron responded firmly yet gently with a shaky, slightly raised voice.

F*ck the Biscuits

"Mum, f*ck the biscuits!"

It's worth pointing out that he has always treated me with respect and would ordinarily never have spoken to me like that. I knew this was serious. Something had happened.

"What is it darling?" I said gently. I was scared to hear his answer, assuming this was going to be more bad news.

In a now quiet and trembling tone, he replied, "I walked today!"

He had done it! I was utterly stunned, I had dreamed of this moment and prayed for it every single day since the accident. There was a heavy and palpable silence. Neither of us spoke a word yet we communicated on such a deep level, completely understanding each other.

Eventually I broke the silence: "You're right, f*ck the biscuits!" was all I could think of to say. Never did I imagine that when I heard the news that every fibre of my being had longed to hear for what felt like an

F*ck the Biscuits

eternity, my response would be "F*ck the biscuits!" There are times when words just don't cut it, and this was one of them. After a period of silence, Aaron told me he needed to call his dad, so I said I'd call him back later when I'd had time to process. "I love you so much," I whispered, as our extraordinary and brief conversation ended.

I was in a complete daze, my head was spinning. Oh my God, he'd done it! My son walked, against all the odds. My hands were trembling, but I had no choice other than to get my act together, there were several somewhat frustrated drivers behind me in the queue and now I needed fuel more than ever, I couldn't wait to get to the unit in the morning. Somehow I managed to start filling my car, Aaron's words whirling round and round in my head: "I walked today." My prayers had been answered. I could feel my emotions rising to the surface, now wasn't the best time but I couldn't hold them back, they were too powerful, too strong. My face crumpled as my eyes blurred.

Desperately trying to hold myself together I made my way to the kiosk, where all I could do was stand and shake. I thought my legs were going to collapse underneath me and I could barely breathe. I was aware of several people around me but the only person I could really see was the woman behind the counter who kindly asked if I was okay. It was then that I discovered I couldn't talk either. She made her way around to me and carefully placed her hand on my arm, signalling to a colleague to find me a chair, at which point I looked her in the face and said, "My son was paralysed in a car accident and he walked for the first time today." This was undoubtedly the single most significant moment of my life and the first person I shared it with was a total stranger. She didn't feel like a stranger though, she felt like my guardian angel.

By now I was sobbing, a tsunami of emotions came flooding out and I couldn't stop it. When I came to my senses, I looked around and saw that I wasn't alone, there were several other customers in tears as they understood the impact that this news had undeniably had on me. They congratulated me and were genuinely happy and interested in our story. The last place I expected to be celebrating was in a petrol station, yet here we were. I felt like I was amongst friends and there was a certain element of intimacy that was shared between us. Having finally paid for my fuel, I returned to my car, but I knew I couldn't drive home until I had calmed down. My vision was still impaired by my tears, so I pulled forward out of the way and sat in my car for some while before I got ready to make my way home.

Finally I was able to safely get behind the wheel, though by now my mind was racing, thinking about all the people to share the good news with, imagining how they would react. Having made it home I walked into my kitchen and had a vivid recollection of the day, comparatively recently, that I had sat at the table that now stood in front of me and whispered, "I wish he would walk." My wish had come true and here I was alone with my thoughts, not quite knowing what to do next.

I called Sue who I knew would be at work, and as she worked at the same Post Office as me, it would kill two birds with one stone. She screamed with pure joy and excitement, then I heard all the cries of elation in the background as the news spread. It was as if everyone there had shared the pain and now they shared the delight. Still smiling and still shaking when I came off the phone, I tried to contact Mark to no avail.

As the reality of what the day had brought us sunk in, it suddenly became too much. I didn't have to fight any more and every emotion I had felt since that fateful day in September spilled out of me. I cried hysterically and held nothing back, to the point where I began to hyperventilate, gasping for breath. I wept oceans. Yet I could not have been happier, this was one the greatest days of my life, second only to the day Aaron was born. I desperately wanted to call Tracy, she was my sister and had been at my side, loving Aaron and supporting us both, she should be one of the first to know. Numerous times I tried to phone her but I couldn't control what was borderline hysteria enough to be able to talk. My hands were trembling and my heart was racing as reality dawned on me. Aaron had walked! Finally, I calmed myself down and called her.

As soon as I heard her voice, I broke down again. I made a futile attempt to explain, but all I could manage to say was "Tracy" in a rasped tone. I was aware that I was scaring her, but it didn't change anything. I couldn't talk. She begged me to tell her what was going on, she even asked me if he was dead, doubtless remembering the episode when he crashed in the operating theatre. Finally, I managed to whisper, "He walked today!" My darling sister said all the right things and totally understood that I couldn't respond. She volunteered to come over and be with me, but I managed to assure her that I was fine. All I had to do was let these emotions come, eventually they would run out of steam, and dissipate in their own time.

Deep down, I was overjoyed and I couldn't begin to imagine how Aaron must be feeling. I was so incredibly proud of him, I still am and I always will be. I was getting tired and needed to conserve my energy to talk to Aaron. I was also concerned that if I heard a kind voice, I might just weaken enough for the hysteria to take hold again so I decided to deliver the news to my closest friends via text message. They understood as I knew they would. My phone quickly became inundated

F*ck the Biscuits

with the most beautiful responses. I felt loved and I felt safe.

My conversation with Aaron later that day was very different to the one we'd had earlier, we shared the excitement and joy as he gave me all the details of what had happened that day. I was eager to get to the hospital, to share his remarkable achievement and to hug him to within an inch of his life! It was tempting to jump in my car and go then but it was a long journey and it was getting late. That pleasure could wait until the morning. On my knees in prayer that night, I expressed my deepest gratitude, before getting into bed and sleeping like a baby.

The next day I had the biggest grin on my face heading towards the hospital, I couldn't have been happier if I tried. When I arrived, there was a buzz in the air and Aaron was keen to get to the gym to show me what he could do and I was eager to see it. He explained that he had walked in a frame, not dissimilar to a baby's walking frame, with a built-in seat if needed. Off we went to the gym, I was so excited, I felt like a child on Christmas morning. We arrived to be told that Georgie was not working that day. Aaron and I looked at each other and the disappointment we both felt was crushing. Then from nowhere another physio appeared, she marched up to Aaron and introduced herself as Sue, telling us that she would be taking Aaron's physio session.

She reminded me of an old-fashioned school PE teacher, slightly abrupt in her mannerism and certainly not one to suffer fools gladly. Aaron started to explain his progress with Georgie and how he wanted to try again in the frame now that I was there. She made it quite clear that the frame was not going to be used that day, and we were both absolutely gutted. She told Aaron and me to follow her to the far end of the gym. Her demeanour was such that it was difficult to argue. Having disappeared into a side room, she left us waiting, feeling so disappointed, confused and deflated... until she returned with crutches in her hand. Neither of us could quite believe what we were seeing, this was huge and, as much as Aaron longed for this level of progress, he didn't feel ready, so he began to explain what he had done thus far with Georgie and how he had only walked in the frame for the first time the day before. Dismissing Aaron's concerns, she suggested that he at least try and, as Aaron is always up for a challenge, he agreed.

Having only once been on his feet with the security of a walking frame, this was not an easy task, but neither Aaron or Sue were prepared to give up and eventually he was upright and, with a belt around his waist to secure him, he took a tentative step forward. I was concerned for his safety at first, he was swaying and teetering to the point of almost falling over, but I had faith that this amazing physio had the situation under control. After a few attempts Aaron was gaining confidence, so she asked if he would like to walk across the gym. The gym is huge and I assumed he would be hesitant, I should have known better: his immediate reply was "Hell yeah!". Sue held on tightly to the belt whilst pushing the wheelchair directly behind him so if he fell he would land in the chair. Not only was this safe but it also gave Aaron much needed assurance. The expression of delight on Aaron's face was a joy. However, this was clearly hard work but his willpower was greater than his need to rest as he pushed forward. Each step must have felt like a mountain to climb as eventually the opposite side of the gym drew closer. By now he had an audience, everyone was watching, this was an unusual sight as sadly the majority of patients don't reach this point.

Just as Aaron neared his goal, Sue said in an upbeat tone, "Fancy walking back to the ward, Aaron?". His ward was some considerable distance from the gym and he immediately hesitated, though his expression quickly changed as he decided to embrace the opportunity. Game on. I walked alongside them, for the most part stunned at what I was witnessing. As we walked down the main corridor leading to the ward, it was obvious that this was becoming an extraordinarily arduous task as the sweat ran from his face and down his neck. He was getting out of breath and looking more and more pale, I was worried that he would collapse and yet still I wanted him to push on. I knew he could, and would, do this. He was so brave, braver than I would have ever been.

F*ck the Biscuits

After what seemed like an eternity, we reached the ward doors which were promptly pulled open by two nurses and we were greeted by both staff and patients alike. This was a phenomenal moment for me, I can only but imagine how Aaron must have felt. It transpired that the ward staff had been briefed and were aware of what was happening. This was not only huge for us, but it was also a momentous occasion for everyone. By now Aaron was literally drenched in sweat, exhausted and breathless. He persevered and walked through the avenue of onlookers, all cheering and applauding, willing him on. He reached his bed and let himself fall on to it, yet he still had the energy to throw his arms in the air and join us all in raucous cheer.

No words could ever describe how proud I felt in that moment, I literally thought I would burst. I had prayed night after night for him to walk again, and to observe and be a part of this incredible success was beyond my wildest dreams. The day before I had sobbed, been hysterical and cried until my tears ran dry. Today I was able to immerse myself in this experience and enjoy it.

There were no tears, instead I smiled and laughed and cheered. It was wonderful. The happiest day of my life was the day Aaron was born, this day came an extremely close second. However, although walking had been the goal, that's not where it ended. This was just the beginning of a long hard journey of emotional and spiritual healing for us both that would last many years.

We later learned that Sue was a physio who specialised in enabling patients to walk, working in spinal units all over the country. She had been drafted in especially to work with Aaron following his pretty miraculous achievements thus far. We never saw her again after that day but my admiration and gratitude for her work will stay with me for the rest of my life. It was after this extraordinary accomplishment that we learned there was something else which had been paramount to Aaron's success.

The following day Steve came to the hospital, he had something he needed to tell Aaron and me. He confessed to us that both the surgeons at Romford Hospital and the team at Stoke Mandeville had categorically told him that Aaron would never walk again. They had said he might get some movement and feeling back, but that he would at no time be able to support his own body weight as there had been too much damage to both the spinal cord and the central nervous system.

Steve then went on to tell us how he went home from Romford that night and sobbed at the devastating news, at which point Cathy had a strong premonition that Aaron would, in fact, walk. Cathy has always been gifted in this way with an extraordinarily accurate psychic ability, having once urgently requested that I tell Tracy she must see a doctor about a scar that would not heal properly near her eyebrow. I took Cathy's advice and it turned out that Tracy had skin cancer, the tissue near her eye was cancerous and dangerously close to her brain. Thanks to Cathy's intervention, Tracy had surgery and went on to make a full recovery. On the night that Steve returned from Romford and told Cathy of Aaron's prognosis she could hear a voice in her head loud and clear telling her that Aaron would walk again.

She explained the one thing that would ensure he walked again was hope, and that it was wrong to take that away from him. They agreed that Aaron should not be told his prognosis and that I should not know either. Steve discussed it with Tracy and Mark who understood and agreed. This explained why my sister had made the banner, she totally got the significance of self-belief and she also understood that the pressure on me would be too great if I knew the truth. They were so very right, during the many times I witnessed Aaron struggling I would not have coped knowing it was likely to be in vain.

The greatest challenge Steve faced was to get the medical professionals to agree to keep this from Aaron. He was twenty-one years old, not a child, and entitled to know the truth. Understanding the impact it would have on Aaron, Steve literally stood in their way when they came to talk to Aaron on his ward at Romford and he begged them not to say anything. He finally compromised, saying that Aaron was mentally in no fit state to receive this news, he was in mourning and shock. Steve agreed to tell him when the time was right. He fought the same battle – unbeknown to me – when Aaron was transferred to Stoke Mandeville, and made the same promise. He fulfilled his promise, Aaron could walk so now was the right time to tell us both that all the doctors said he would never walk again!

This was ABSOLUTELY HUGE with an enormous and valuable lesson. I completely get the ethical dilemma of giving anyone false hope, but no-one has the right to take away an individual's hope. I will always believe that there are many patients past, present and future who will spend the rest of their lives in a wheelchair simply because that's what they've been told. It becomes a self-fulfilling prophecy.

It was just before Aaron was finally discharged from the spinal unit when he was asked to go back to Romford Hospital to see Mr. David who was the consultant in charge of his care there, and was the lead surgeon who operated on his spine. When we walked into his consulting room, he looked up at Aaron and the look on his face was memorable, bordering on comical, he was clearly shocked to see just how well

Aaron could walk. He told us that he was aware of the fact that Aaron was walking but he had no idea just how mobile he was. He then went on to tell us that if he had not seen this with his own eyes then he would not have believed it, based on what he saw on the operating table and all the subsequent scans and tests he had believed that this was simply not medically possible. I rest my case when it comes to the power of the mind. We left that room on a high, we had heard it from the horse's mouth... Aaron had walked against all the odds and, yet again, my pride swelled. I felt a huge sense of relief that our journey had taken us to this point and was riding on a high.

Having hope is important to the very act of being a human being. As Dr. Judith Rich, a pioneering teacher in the field of transformation and consciousness, writes: "Hope is a match in a dark tunnel, a moment of light, just enough to reveal the path ahead and ultimately the way out." Hope is about positive beliefs when we have a clear goal in mind. It's about a belief that we can overcome challenges and adversity. It was the key that unlocked Aaron's potential. Hope gives you motivation. It's the voice inside that says, "Yes, you can." It's that voice that makes you work hard and gives you the impetus to try. I truly believe that the combination of Steve's intervention and the use of visualisation techniques is the reason Aaron walked, and is where he is today.

Hope is being able to see that there is light, despite of all the darkness.

Desmond Tutu

Cathy was familiar with visualisation techniques, how they work and how potent they are. The mind is a powerful healing tool. Imagery, or visualisation, has harnessed the power of the mind through various therapies for centuries. I read an interesting article in a publication called Spinal Journal written by a neuroscientist in New Delhi in which he discusses visualisation. He states that mental imagery has been studied in various neurological conditions such as stroke and spinal cord injury and has been seen to be effective in bringing about functional gains - that is, increases in strength and mobility. He goes on to say that science proves that the relevant brain activity and motor functions are present when patients generate mental imagery.

David Hamilton, who obtained an honours degree in biological and medicinal chemistry, and a Ph.D. in organic chemistry, before working as a scientist in the pharmaceutical industry for several years, stated: "Since 2006 visualisation has shown positive results in spinal injury rehabilitation. Patients use their minds to imagine moving normally, and the moment they do so, the arm or leg that they envision in motion, is stimulated at a microscopic level, and the brain area that governs each limb is also triggered. The result is that over time their movements improve. In stroke cases, some damaged brain areas even begin to regenerate. The placebo effect has shown us for years that the power of belief can influence the course of an entire range of medical conditions, and even alter immunity and growth hormone levels. Research has shown that when people take a placebo and believe it to be real medicine, chemical shifts occur in the brain. Now we know for certain based on scientific research that thoughts, emotions and beliefs aren't just subjective ideas in the mind, but that they cause real physical and chemical changes in the brain and throughout the body."

Deep down I knew that I had buried my head in the sand to avoid facing any prognosis the professionals along our journey thus far might have offered. At any point I could have simply enquired, but the words of my late mother must have subconsciously been with me. She used to say, "Never ask a question unless you're prepared to hear the answer." So I never asked.

Aaron loved the physio gym even more now, and was in there practising on his crutches whenever he could. He was under strict instructions not to use, or even take, the crutches outside of the gym, unless under the supervision of a physio.

Did they not know Aaron by now?

I sat in what was Jimmy's cafe one day waiting for him, I wasn't sure where he was, which was nothing unusual. I glanced through the long glass window that looked out onto the corridor linking the wards to the gym, only to see Aaron wheeling himself at full speed, as if his life depended on it, with a pair of crutches over his lap. He was going so fast, he looked like he was in some kind of paralympic relay race with crutches as the baton. The sight was hilarious and as I met him at the end of the corridor, he said, "Mum, don't just stand there laughing, help me. I've stolen these crutches." We somehow managed to sneak them onto the ward, and from that day on whenever he thought no-one was around, he would practise walking on them. In truth they must have known, but like so many other things with Aaron, they turned a blind eye. They saw the fire in Aaron, they had seen where it had got him, and they were no longer going to stand in his way. Aaron had earned the right to break the rules.

His weekend visits to Steve's continued, he would have his wheelchair but practise his mobility in the safety of Steve's home whenever he could, and it was slowly improving with time. Because Steve was stronger and able to catch Aaron if, and when, he fell, it was an ideal environment for this. Friends and family would visit,

F*ck the Biscuits

allowing Aaron to show them his progress. To say he was surrounded by love, encouragement and support is an understatement.

At the time, Steve and Cathy had a black labrador by the name of Tilly who would ordinarily sleep upstairs at night, but because Aaron had to sleep downstairs Tilly would stay with him all through the night, she rarely left his side, as if she knew how tough it was for him. Dogs are extraordinary animals, instinctively knowing when someone they love is in distress. It was about a year later that Aaron fell in love with a black labrador puppy, he bought her and named her Mia. She quickly became his best friend. Over the years Aaron has often said that Mia was there for him during his darkest times. In return she has had a wonderful life. As I write, Mia is still with us, she's an old girl now but is still at Aaron's side.

By now Steve and I had become aware that there was another issue which needed to be dealt with. Aaron had always had a close relationship with Heather and she had been incredibly supportive and understanding considering everything she was having to contend and come to terms with. Inevitably though, her journey was to take a different direction. She was innocent to the fact that she was indeed holding Aaron back, there were times when he seemed to be moving forward with his grief. He would laugh, have days when he felt good and was definitely making progress. Then Heather would call or visit and inadvertently drag him down again, leaving him feeling guilty and lonely. He had to try and move on and she was nowhere near ready for that. Heather was leaning on him, and I also think that being with Aaron made her feel closer to Olivia and Jack. This was perfectly understandable. Excuse the pun but Aaron would take two steps forward then Heather would inadvertently pull him one step back.

We had to take action, as parents we had to do what was right for our child when he was not in a position to think clearly for himself. Steve spoke to Heather, sadly I don't think she really understood and I get that. This poor woman, we were taking away a support system that she badly needed. But Aaron was not strong enough to be that support. I found the whole thing incredibly difficult. The last thing we wanted to do was cause her more pain but there was no doubt that it had to be done. It would have been easier to have buried our heads in the sand and hope the problem would resolve itself, but the easy option is not always the right one, and I am pretty sure the problem would have escalated without our intervention.

Christmas Day was fast approaching and my darling sister had organised for her, my brother-in-law Karl, and my nephews Josh and Rory to spend Christmas Day at the spinal unit. At the time my nephews were only two and four years old. What an incredible thing to do, to effectively give up your Christmas Day to spend it in hospital when you have young children. It was a powerful show of love not just on Tracy's part but from Karl too. For anyone feeling a bit sorry for the children at this point, rest assured they enjoyed their adventure and their parents put on a big Christmas Day for them at home the following day.

We had also agreed to bring Aaron back to his dad's that night for a few days. It's easy to question why go to all that trouble, why not just let Aaron spend Christmas Day at his dad's? The answer is simple yet painful, Aaron was distraught and not coping with Christmas at all. He didn't want to face the outside world or to acknowledge Christmas in any way. We had to take the softly, softly approach.

En route to the unit that morning Aaron called me, he was sobbing hysterically and begged me not to come, and to tell Tracy and Karl not to come either. He explained through tears of pain and sorrow that it was not fair on the boys, he couldn't be strong in front of them. If you thought we were going to leave you alone to deal with this Aaron, think again! I reassured him that everyone understood the trauma he was feeling, and that there were enough of us to take care of the boys. Despite Aaron's wishes, we all met at the hospital for what was to be a long, emotional and interesting day.

By the time we arrived Aaron had calmed down a little, but one look at his face gave me an insight into the pain he was feeling. He looked so small and vulnerable, with incredible sadness in his eyes and demeanour.

F*ck the Biscuits

Aaron had his own side room, complete with a wetroom for wheelchair access. As I walked in, he was having his blood pressure taken by a pirate – all the staff had dressed in fancy dress for the day, at least this was something to amuse the children. Aaron again begged me to tell Tracy and Karl not to come, but I explained that they were almost there and reassured him that if he couldn't cope, we'd just have a coffee and they would go home. This seemed to work, the pressure was off. Aaron wheeled himself into the wetroom for a quick wash, not long after which Tracy, Karl and the boys appeared. I was both relieved and anxious to see them, I needed them to be there badly, but I wasn't sure how Aaron would deal with it. His head was all over the place.

Just as I was pondering all of this, he called to Tracy and Karl from the bathroom, asking them to come over. "Watch this," he said, and with that he slowly and deliberately walked across the wetroom towards them. My heart was in my mouth, he padded slowly and was a little wobbly. I was so scared that he would fall but I knew better than to stand in his way. He did it, the mood quickly changed and when I looked across, both Tracy and Karl were crying. They were amazed. Aaron's demeanour had changed and he looked so incredibly pleased with himself, why wouldn't he? Karl summed it up as he wiped his eyes and quietly said, "That is the best Christmas present I have ever had."

From then on, the atmosphere changed, it felt uplifted and Aaron's intense anxiety had dissipated. He did have a few moments during the day when he got quite tearful but by then he felt comfortable enough to do so without fear of judgement. We all got it, even the young boys weren't perturbed by it. Steve and I had been trying to persuade Aaron to come home to his dad's for Christmas but Aaron was not willing to commit. He couldn't face everyone having a good time, and he certainly wasn't in the mood to have any fun, or indeed to feel good about anything. His grief was far too raw.

Steve and I were worried about him being in the hospital on his own, most of his mates had gone home for the holidays, but we decided not to push it. Aaron could do whatever he felt he needed to. We had a buffet lunch that Tracy had brought along, served from a physio bed covered in a festive tablecloth, and offered to share it with other patients and staff. Tracy had made a real effort with the food and I was extremely grateful. It was the strangest Christmas party or Christmas day I have ever experienced and yet it felt comfortable and right under the circumstances. We exchanged gifts and played with the boys who, by now, were running round the wards spotting all the various characters that the staff were dressed up as, much to the delight of everyone. Children make Christmas special and this day was no different.

Every so often, Aaron would open up and talk about how he was feeling, it was reassuring to know that he felt relaxed enough to do this. It was also heartbreaking to witness his pain, you could see it in his eyes and hear it in his voice. The day brought a mixture of gratitude, heartbreak and sorrow for both Aaron and me. My thoughts kept leading back to Heather and wondering how the day must be for her, I'm not sure anyone could ever know.

As the afternoon passed, Tracy and Karl got ready to take the boys home. Then, to my astonishment and delight, Aaron asked if he could come home with us. I called Steve to give him the good news, and to tell him to expect us in a few hours. We packed up, cleared his leave with the nursing team and got Aaron's things together. This included his beloved crutches which by now rarely left his side.

We got to Steve's by early evening, the whole family was there, including Aaron's brother and sisters, eagerly awaiting his arrival. Not only was Aaron welcomed with love and warmth, Mark and I were too. The intention had been to settle Aaron at his dad's then make our way home, but we ended up staying until really late, enjoying a great deal of wine and food. We played games and laughed, the atmosphere was incredibly relaxed, and it was just the therapy that Aaron needed. I realised that I was desperate to simply chill out and relax too. Christmas 2008 will go down for me as the strangest, emotionally the toughest and yet the most memorable one I have ever had. What an extraordinary year it had been.

F*ck the Biscuits

After the holidays we took Aaron back to the spinal unit, he was feeling ready to embrace the challenges ahead, get stuck into his rehab and physio which of course had taken on a whole new meaning now, and get himself fit and strong. There is an amazing concept at the spinal unit: a purpose-built bungalow on site, designed to be wheelchair friendly but with no hospital equipment at all. Each patient is required to spend a night or weekend in the bungalow as part of their rehabilitation to see how they would cope at home. It was funded by donations from a very grateful relative and I thought it was a superb idea.

Early in the new year, Aaron and Eddie were allocated a weekend in the bungalow. So, they were going to let these two loose in there for a couple of nights, brave move. They were excited and wanted me to take them to the nearest supermarket to stock up on essentials - beer and steak. This turned out to be absolutely hilarious, there was never a dull moment when they got together. By this time Aaron's walking had improved considerably so he didn't want to take his wheelchair, and he got in the back of the car while

Eddie transferred himself into the front seat. The wheels of Eddie's chair then slid off so I could fold it and put it in the boot. All good so far.

We got to the supermarket, I got Eddie's chair for him - put one wheel on but couldn't get the other one on. The car I had at the time was not the greatest, it was a three-door vehicle and only the passenger's seat would go down for access to the back so Aaron couldn't get out to help me. Instead of getting stressed, we all started to get a fit of the giggles. They were laughing at my expense, as I struggled to get the second wheel on, until in the end I smirked and looked at Eddie and said, "I don't know why you're laughing, I only brought you along so I could use the disabled parking space." This made him laugh even more, it may appear on the face of it to be in bad taste, but it wasn't. I believe it's known as laughing in the face of adversity and it works wonders at times. Humour is good for the soul and it's not always easy for me to relay a lot of the laughs we had along our journey, but trust me when I say we did.

Eventually I managed to click the wheel safely in place, and we were ready to shop. We made our way around the aisles, Eddie in his chair and Aaron walking slowly. As we waited at the checkout, I suddenly realised why the woman on the till was giving us such a filthy look. Aaron could walk but, as yet, he couldn't stand very well. His balance was all over the place and he was not able to stand without wobbling and having to hold on tight to any surface to stop himself falling over. He looked completely drunk. We must have seemed a strange sight, the three of us. I didn't care, it was so good and such a tonic to see these two young men enjoying life, albeit temporarily. We made our way back to the unit and I carried their shopping to the bungalow, so happy for them. I left them to it, that was after all the whole point of the exercise. Oh to have been a fly on the wall... I hope they both look back on that weekend with some fond memories, even though it was possibly the darkest period of their lives.

Aaron was eventually discharged and five months after the prognosis that he would never walk again, he walked unaided from the Spinal Unit in February 2009.

For most of the journey thus far, that very concept had been beyond anything I dared to wish for. It was an emotional day, we took an enormous bouquet for Georgie and lots of chocolates for the staff. We paid a visit to the gym before leaving, with lots of hugs and tears from Georgie and the other physios. The hospital had become our home from home, we had made so many friends there. This was a special case, this is not the outcome for the majority of patients, so the hospital PR department had arranged for a photographer to take pictures of us. Aaron had become a bit of a celebrity in the unit and they wanted to celebrate his success. Driving home felt exciting and yet a little scary. Life had taken an enormous detour, leaving the unit was not the end of the story, we knew that, but we didn't really know what to expect next. Aaron had a way to go with his recovery on so many levels, he might have no longer been surrounded by the safety and security of a medical team, but he was engulfed in love. And love will always find a way.

Having moved in with Steve and Cathy following his discharge, Aaron found life very strange to begin with but was welcomed with open arms by everyone. It felt good to have him living so much closer and was a welcome relief to know that he was safe and cared for. I'm not suggesting that this wasn't the case in the spinal unit, but knowing his family and those who love him were around all the time felt very different. I would visit regularly and we often went out for lunch together, in many ways they were good times even if somewhat surreal. Up until then this had not been our reality, so it took a while to get used to a different lifestyle.

As time passed it became apparent that there was another underlying issue that would need to be dealt with. Weeks would pass without Aaron coming to visit me, despite many offering to take him there, it was obvious after a while that he was avoiding coming to what was his family home up until that fateful night in September. I didn't have the facilities to accommodate him in the short term as he was still not able to climb stairs, but with the passing of time this was improving so he could have potentially worked towards this.

There was a far more disturbing reason why he wasn't able to return to our house, his home. Memories.

The house reminded Aaron of the life that he had lost. In one extraordinary turn of fate he had lost his girlfriend and best friend, his mobility and his career, along with his confidence and sense of belonging. His life had been ripped out from underneath him and going home was evocative of that existence and too painful to bear. I found this so difficult, the thought that my own son couldn't bring himself to come to our home; the place where he had grown up which had once held warm and loving memories now haunted him. It didn't seem fair to either of us.

I sat quietly at home one day, reminiscing about how life used to be before the accident. How happy the house was, despite a few arguments and disagreements along the way. At that moment I wanted it all back, just to be normal again and to see him walk through the door. The tears ran down my face and neck as I longed for something that I knew wasn't going to happen. The house was quiet, it had lost its energy and no longer felt like home. I was worried for Aaron, how must this feel for him? Being unable to face the trauma of coming home. What was once a sanctuary was now a scary place for him to be. My heart broke for him. Yet again I was left with that all too familiar feeling of helplessness, I couldn't fix this either.

One morning I got a phone call from Cathy to say that she was bringing Aaron over, she wanted to make sure I would be in. Initially I was thrilled until she explained that he did not know, she planned to take him for a drive and just come over. We agreed that he needed to face his demons and we mums had to take control and make this happen, forcing the issue was the only way. I knew she was right but if, when he arrived, he couldn't bring himself to come in I was not going to make him. Despite the plan being the only way forward it still felt wrong and I was worried for Aaron - nothing new there then. An hour or so later they arrived. Aaron sat in the car and I went out to meet him, he wasn't angry at being coerced, he understood but he was so anxious. My heart was racing, I could see the look of fear in Aaron's eyes. Our home was once full of happy memories, this felt so wrong.

He got out of the car while Cathy and I tried to be as casual as was possible under the circumstances. I said I would pop the kettle on and invited them both to come in. He got as far as the door and froze, he shot me a terrified look and said, "Mum, I can't do this."

Having faced far worse over the last six months, I knew he could. I gently took his hand, smiled with love and warmth, and said, "Yes you can."

His hand was shaking in mine as I led him through the back door into the kitchen. Now that he had crossed the threshold he calmed down slightly and took a seat at the table. We had done it, and my son had finally walked through the door that I often would look at and picture him coming through. He didn't breeze through in the way that I had imagined, but this was still happening and it was at least some progress.

After a fashion Aaron calmed down, he relaxed a little then to my surprise he decided to take a look around the house. He went into the lounge then into his bedroom, I knew this would be the hardest part. Olivia and Jack had spent so much time in that room with him, although I had already sorted through and discreetly stored away any items which I thought would be too difficult for him to see for the time being, such as cards from Olivia and Jack's CDs. Hopefully that worked because, although he was very tearful, his anxiety seemed to have abated. Another hurdle had been overcome. Aaron and Cathy stayed for a cup of tea, we chatted and relaxed for a while before they left and I truly believed we had crossed a bridge and that things would simply go back to normal. I was wrong. Aaron didn't visit again for some while.

It was several months later when I was woken by Mark at about 2 o'clock in the morning to say we had a visitor. I knew immediately who he meant, and ran downstairs to find Aaron in the kitchen. He fell into my arms and sobbed. Having been out for the evening with his friends, he had called Mark to take him home to me, he was at such a low ebb. Everything had come crashing down and overwhelmed him. I held him tight until he eventually pulled back slightly to look me in the eyes and told me that he simply felt so lonely. It was like a knife through my heart, his pain was my pain. I promised him that he would never be alone while I was in this world, I meant it then and I still do. We ended up talking quietly on the sofa while Aaron ate the sandwich that I had made him. The desperation to see me was stronger than the fear and pain of being at our home, and was enough to help him turn a corner. From that night he would often come over, though deep down I knew that he would never live there again.

Another challenge was looming, we now had a date for the coroner's inquest which was held at Chelmsford Court. What a day that was, and not one I would want to repeat in a hurry.

Steve and I took Aaron, who was feeling extremely nervous about having to make his statement. His main concern was that he didn't want Olivia to be deemed responsible for the accident in any way, and of course today was going to bring some traumatic memories to the surface. When we arrived, we were taken to a large room and met by the police and a representative of the court. Aaron was unaware that one of the reasons we were taken to a separate room was that Michael had arrived and was on a mission to find and blame Aaron for what had happened. I knew this was going to happen. Everyone did their best to keep the atmosphere calm, and to keep Aaron in the dark about Michael.

I don't really remember all the details but I will doubtless never forget how stressed and vulnerable Aaron looked. In court, he was asked to recall every single detail leading up to the crash and to the moment of impact. Can you imagine how that must have felt for him? The coroner was very caring though, regularly asking if he needed a break or a drink of water. All the time I was acutely aware of Michael's presence, I could feel it even when I wasn't looking at him. Heather was there too, she had the appearance of a broken woman and I suspect that's just how she felt. Michael wanted to ask a question, for which he was given an opportunity. My heart was racing, concerned that he would directly implicate Aaron, not because I thought for one moment that the coroner would see it that way but because of the effect it would have on Aaron's state of mind.

Michael didn't, he simply asked if the accident was caused by 'someone' pulling on the handbrake. The police were able to confirm with absolutely no doubt that this was not the case. With that he simply thanked them and left the stand, he now looked broken and, despite everything, my heart went out to him. We never heard from him again.

The coroner confirmed a verdict of accidental death and no-one involved was deemed responsible. This was an incredible relief for everyone concerned. Aaron had another legal process which was ongoing, and that was the insurance compensation claim. It was a process that took a considerably long time and was finally settled many years after the accident. It was in a boardroom in the financial district of London where I cried unashamedly as all parties agreed on a figure, as I believed that justice had been done and the nightmare was finally over. I was naive and didn't realise then that, in truth, it will never really be over.

CHAPTER NINE

Giving Back

My prayers had, without a shadow of a doubt, been answered. With each and every prayer, I promised to give something back if only Aaron could walk and now was the time to fulfil that promise.

Whilst we were at Stoke Mandeville, I came across a charity known as Spinal Research. They are the UK's leading charity funding research around the world to develop effective treatments and ultimately a cure for Spinal Cord Injury, believing in a future where to have this type of injury is no longer a life sentence. As we now truly understood the impact that Spinal Cord Injury has on lives, it seemed an obvious way to pay my debt of gratitude.

From the very beginning of our journey the press had shown a great deal of interest in our story, so I decided it was time to put my thinking cap on and figure out

F*ck the Biscuits

how to utilise this for the good of others. My amazing group of friends offered their support and so a team of helpers was born, and together we were determined to raise as much money as we could.

Ideas came in thick and fast and one of the first events was an evening of live music with a hog roast, which affectionately became known as the Gig and Pig! A friend of mine is the lead singer in a band called Stiff in the Morning (yes, that really is their name and they're absolutely awesome), he and the band volunteered to play for free and provide the hog roast at cost price. By this time, I was back at work in the village post office which proved to be the perfect platform to publicise our events and so very much more. The gig was a sell out, the band did not disappoint, they made it a really fun night. Everyone danced the night away and enjoyed the food. People left with happy smiling faces and, I'm pleased to say, empty wallets.

As we went on to do at all of our events, we held a raffle. The community soon got to hear that we were fundraising and people were generous with their prize

Giving Back

donations. It was almost on a daily basis that gifts would either be brought to my place of work or to my home, which is how we came to have some incredible raffle prizes on the night and I was going to make sure they added considerably to our total. I've spoken about my dear friend Jan, not only had she been an unbelievable support to us all in her own special way but she had another asset which was worth putting to use... she's a buxom wench is our Jan so I suggested she put her assets to good use and chat the men up to part with their cash. It worked, she wouldn't take no for an answer, and we made a fortune on the raffle. It was all done in good spirits, everyone was more than happy to help.

Aaron and I got up on stage while the band took a break to thank everyone for their love and support, we were received with applause and cheers. It felt good, so completely different to the dark times we had faced. I don't remember how much we made on the night, but I do remember being astounded by people's generosity. Doing something so positive in every way felt right, I

F*ck the Biscuits

was exhausted, slightly drunk and on top of the world by the time we made our way home.

Tracy and Karl are keen golfers so they suggested we organise a charity golf day at their club. This turned out to be a very lucrative idea. One of the biggest challenges was to get decent prizes to cover all the different categories for the competitors. People were happy to pay good money for the day but, rightly so, they expected the best in return. No pressure then. So I made it my mission to chat up all the local business owners who turned out to be extremely generous. There were beautiful bouquets for the ladies, weekends away, someone had a villa in Portugal and they were kind enough to donate a week's stay there, meals at some wonderful restaurants and bottles of expensive wine galore, plus lots more…

We had enough but I didn't turn away any offers which is how we came to have ample donations to hold an auction on the day too. My late father was an auctioneer, I've no doubt he would have loved it and been very proud of our achievements. Spinal Research had shown considerable interest in our fundraising so

Giving Back

they provided official banners and merchandise, and even sent a representative along to talk about the work they do. The day was another huge success, I was buzzing for several days afterwards and my phone didn't stop ringing. In fact, it was such a triumph that we went on to hold another three at various clubs. We were on a roll... what could we do next?

Jan heard about an abseiling charity event being held locally and suggested we get a team together. I was more than happy to recruit willing, brave souls to take the plunge but with my fear of heights there was no way I was going to climb down the side of an extremely high building. My role was to be the co-ordinator with my feet firmly on the ground. The team consisted of eight women, one of whom was Sandra who was a good friend and I had known her for years. She told me that she too had a fear of heights but wanted to overcome this and give it a try. My team were tireless in their efforts to get sponsorship and when the day arrived there was a lot of money riding on their courage. They looked good in their Spinal Research T-

F*ck the Biscuits

shirts, lots of people came to cheer them on and the atmosphere was buzzing.

A few of the girls were understandably a little anxious, but we were all concerned for one of our team members, Sandra. She was absolutely terrified. I took her to one side and reassured her that she really did not have to go through with it but she was having none of it. Having spent so many months watching with admiration as Aaron faced considerable fears and challenges, I found myself doing the same as we watched Sandra begin her descent which didn't go as well as it could have done. She bounced against the wall and at one point was hanging in mid-air by which time I think we had all stopped breathing. Eventually she made it down, she was crying and shaking violently. The organisers asked her husband to come through the safety barrier to be with her and medics kept a careful eye on her. My heart went out to Sandra and it swelled with pride, once she had calmed down her face beamed. What an amazing achievement, she must have felt so good. I write this in Loving Memory of her as she sadly lost her life to illness some years

Giving Back

later. She was undeniably brave, funny, determined, kind and a very special woman who lives on in our hearts.

One of my favourite events was a ladies driving challenge that was held on an airbase in Suffolk and once again a team of volunteers was assembled, myself included this time, I wasn't going to miss this opportunity. With lots of sponsorship depending on our success we again looked the part in our Spinal Research outfits as our exciting day began. We drove 4x4 vehicles, enormous American style HGVs, tractors, go carts, racing cars and diggers. It was so much fun, if a little scary at times. Personally I enjoyed the 4x4 course the most but the HGV terrified me, the air was blue by the time I climbed down from the driver's seat! I'd always fancied driving a lorry, but rest assured I'll never do it again. Once more we had raised a great deal of money and had also raised awareness of the charity with our banners and outfits. There was only one thing left to do, head for the nearest pub to celebrate our success.

F*ck the Biscuits

Family, friends, the community and total strangers were incredibly generous and supportive in every way possible. As a result we had raised just over an amazing £10,000. I was thrilled at the incredible amount of money, and I had fulfilled the promise I made in my prayers, I had given something back.

By now I was getting used to seeing Aaron's picture on newspaper stands in shops and supermarkets. The media showed a lot of interest in both our work and Aaron's story, so each time they wanted to do an article the answer was always only on the proviso that they included Spinal Research, explaining the work they do and how to donate. Aaron was interviewed on a couple of radio stations too. I contacted our local ITV television station and offered them the opportunity to tell Aaron's story on the same proviso, which they jumped at. Filming took place both at my home and in the village where I lived, the result was a heart-warming story of hope and determination with gratefully received publicity for Spinal Research. The piece also spoke about the fact that Mark and I were to finally marry, having postponed our wedding because

Giving Back

of the accident. On the evening it was aired my phone didn't stop ringing with people congratulating us on the success of our fundraising and, of course, in praise and awe of Aaron for his remarkable achievement.

Fourteen years later I learned that an old friend of mine had seen me on television and felt inspired to write a poem...

PROUD MUM

I saw you on the telly

Talking of your son

The number one man in your life

That's your Aaron

The warmth in your voice

The love in your eyes

The smile on your face

The joy in your heart

To walk down the aisle

You thought you may not see

With a smile on your face

F*ck the Biscuits

With tears in your eyes
To walk down the aisle
This you will see
A Loving Mum
A Caring Mum
A Loving Son
A Proud Mum

Bill Ormsby

Now it was time to move on, an astonishing amount of money and awareness had been raised. Our story had been told far and wide from many perspectives. It was over, time to move forward and time for Aaron to rebuild his life. But would it ever really be over?

CHAPTER TEN

It Never Really Ends

Having lived at his dad's for some while, Aaron bought his first house in the summer of 2009. It was in need of some care and love but otherwise an ideal home. Before he moved in, I cleaned it from top to bottom, both because Aaron was a little susceptible to infection as he was still using a catheter and because it was something I could do for him so I was grateful to be able to help.

He rented out one room to his brother Sam, and another to his close friend Ant. They were such fun times, at long last Aaron could begin to enjoy life again and he did. There were several parties and boys' nights in. They were all in their early twenties, full of fun and energy, and the house had an energy to match. I used to love going round there, we always had a laugh and occasionally I would stay overnight so I could have a few cheeky glasses of wine. Good times at long last.

F*ck the Biscuits

Aaron hosted Christmas for the family in his new home, which was a world apart from the year before spent in the spinal unit. There was a great deal of love, laughter and extremely good food. Aaron learned to cook at a fairly young age and Ant is an excellent cook so between them they produced a feast fit for a king. We stayed up until the wee small hours playing games, laughing and enjoying this new reality. It was perfect despite everything. I have some wonderful memories of time spent in that house and often reflect back on them as the good old days.

Aaron continued to work hard to improve his mobility and made great progress. He was still not fit to work which he found incredibly frustrating, but in honesty I was happy to be able to visit often and spend time together. In those days I was a keen gardener and was having a tidy-up one day, our shed was full of Aaron's bits and pieces so I asked him, as his shed was much bigger than mine, if he could come over and take it all away. He turned up a few days later with a van and Sam to help. I was sitting in the garden while they were busy in the shed when I heard a great deal of commotion only to look up in time to see them both running away. I couldn't believe my eyes, Aaron was running. It may have been clumsy but he was definitely running, I couldn't believe what I was seeing and my heart missed a beat as I watched in awe and, frankly, shock. Unbeknown to me, Aaron had been practising this and he just wanted to get a little quicker before showing me but the wasps' nest they stumbled on changed his plan!

Be under no illusion, there were dark times too. Aaron was still grieving and facing a great deal of medical issues on a daily basis. He was in pain at times, and struggling with bowel and bladder issues which included using a catheter himself every time he needed the toilet. I would often look at him and feel so sorry for him, there were times when it felt like everything was an uphill task and I wished I could give him a break from it all. One day we would laugh, the next we would cry. That's how life was.

His friends were incredibly supportive and accepting of the situation, taking it in their stride. We all went to a family party with live music which was a wonderful

F*ck the Biscuits

night, we danced the night away and had a great time. During the evening I saw Aaron go into the toilets and had a gut feeling that something was wrong. Then I noticed several of his friends disappearing in the same direction, by which time I knew something was not right. I was worried and was about to go and find out what was going on when they appeared together from the toilets where they had all gathered. They were all covered in soaking wet patches so I asked them what on earth was happening. They explained that Aaron had wet himself and was, understandably, upset which is why they had all splashed each other in a water fight so that Aaron wouldn't stand out. If Aaron was wet, they were all going to be wet. After laughing and congratulating them on their initiative, I took myself away to shed a few silent tears. For me, this simple act epitomised the value of true friendship and it touched my heart.

Unfortunately, having 'accidents' where toilet issues are concerned was a fairly regular occurrence in the early days of recovery. This affected Aaron's confidence, particularly when he went out, but his

It Never Really Ends

friends stood by him and supported him in every way. I would constantly try to reassure him that it was okay and that it would improve. In truth I wasn't entirely sure if it would improve but I was not going to let Aaron see my doubt.

Wherever he went he always had a rucksack on him with catheters, sanitising hand gel, pads and clean clothes. I hated that he had to do this, a young man of his age should be carefree. But, as ever, I couldn't change it for him and was only ever able to love him and help him face the challenges. I remember being at a small, local festival with Aaron and his friends the following summer. As usual he had his essentials in a rucksack. As he needed to change his catheter, he was cleaning his hands with the gel when one of his mates started taking the mickey out of him. He meant no harm, his other friends took him to one side to explain why Aaron was using the hand gel at which point he was absolutely mortified. He had no idea that Aaron used the gel for this purpose, nor indeed that he used a catheter every time he needed the toilet. No harm was done and the issue was quickly resolved, until the next time when another situation would doubtless arise.

Life went on with all its ups and downs, then about eighteen months after the accident Tracy and Karl decided to take the children to Disneyland in Florida and asked if Mark and I would like to join them. A holiday was long overdue so we said we would take them up on their offer, at which point Karl suggested that Mark and I get married there. We had postponed our wedding when the accident happened and had not got as far as re-organising it. My heart hadn't been in it, I associated the wedding with the accident so to go abroad and get married seemed like an ideal solution.

We booked a wedding chapel in Florida who sorted everything for us, we were good to go. It would be an intimate affair with just Tracy, Karl and the children who were to be little page boys. Or paper boys as Josh excitedly told everyone much to our amusement. I really wanted Aaron to be there too, I secretly thought and hoped he would fly over to surprise me but, as the time got nearer, I needed to know if he was coming. My heart wouldn't let me get married without him. He told me that he had booked a flight, there was no way he would miss it. Everything was coming together at long last and I was about to get my happy ending.

We were in Florida a week before the wedding and Aaron joined us the day before. During the week we went to a local diner and I got chatting to the waitress, telling her all about Aaron and how we were finally getting married with Aaron walking me down the aisle. She was fascinated and we talked for ages, I laughed that we had nothing to do, and nowhere organised to go, after the wedding. She literally ran to get the boss to tell him the story. He was mesmerized and asked if we would like to go there for a meal afterwards saying that they would make it look nice for us. We took him up on his offer, and were not disappointed.

The place where we got married was called the 'Stay Happy Stay In Love Wedding Chapel' and was as cheesy as its name, but we had a lot of fun with it. The day was basically run by one woman who resembled Cruella Deville and was almost as scary. She was dishing out orders to everyone involved but would never quite finish what she was saying before disappearing again. It was hilarious, we were all confused but giggling and enjoying the novelty factor.

Finally the time came, Aaron and I walked arm-in-arm down the beautiful aisle to the sound of soft music. We looked at each other, both knowing how hard the journey had been for us both to get to this point. I felt a lump in my throat, the emotions rising in me. I was so blessed to have Aaron by my side, the road that led us to where we were in that moment had been crazy. I couldn't have been happier, though on reflection that was more about sharing this day with Aaron. The officiant was a wonderful man and conducted a truly lovely service. He had lived in the UK, very near to where we lived, before moving to Florida a number of years previously, small world as they say.

After the service we made our way back to the diner as arranged. We travelled in a limo with champagne on board and when we reached our destination I couldn't believe what I was seeing. An enormous balloon arch had been assembled across the entrance with a machine blowing bubbles over us as we walked through. Inside was an incredible transformation, the table was laid to perfection with so many decorations. It was just like a well thought out wedding reception, and certainly not something put together in only two days. The drinks and laughter flowed, everyone had a good time and eventually we made our way back to the villa we were all sharing. I was utterly and completely exhausted, I hadn't felt like that in a while. Mark wanted to go out and continue the celebrations but I didn't have an ounce of energy left so he went out with Aaron, Tracy and Karl while I stayed back to babysit. With the boys tucked up in their beds, I pretty much collapsed onto the settee, then it hit me and it hit hard. Every single emotion I had felt since that fateful day when our lives changed forever rose up from the depths of me. That was how I came to spend my wedding night alone, weeping oceans. Little did I know then that, some fourteen years later, my marriage would end the same way it began.

When we got back home, I decided to take the opportunity to get one more big publicity push for Spinal Research so I contacted the local newspaper who said they would be thrilled to cover the story, my happy ending after being told that Aaron would never walk again to him being able to walk me down the aisle. However, it turned out not to be my happy ending, just the beginning of another chapter in my life. They produced a double page article with our pictures on the front cover. It was quite surreal seeing my wedding photo on the front of the paper in the newsstands but the awareness raised for Spinal Research was well worth it.

It wasn't long after this that Aaron told me he wanted to take a trip to Australia with a couple of his friends. They were to get a three-month visa and travel along the Gold Coast. Understandably I had my reservations, simply because of his health and fitness level, but his friends assured me that they would take care of him. And I knew they would. Before long Aaron and two of his friends were standing in his lounge with their backpacks, waiting for a taxi to take them to Heathrow Airport. There was a great deal of excitement in the air and I knew this could be exactly what Aaron needed to get him to the next level. I was obviously a little sad to see him go, but was really happy for him.

It Never Really Ends

We kept in touch via social media and the occasional telephone call. It was on one of these calls that Aaron told me that he had met a young woman by the name of Amy. She was also travelling with friends, on a one-year visa which she was about half way through. The timing wasn't great to get too involved in a relationship so they went their separate ways. However, they kept in touch and met up again before Aaron returned to the UK.

There's never a dull moment in Aaron's life, and I was somewhat shocked to see a post on Facebook one day saying he was to take part in a Skydive the following day. I jokingly told him that wasn't the way I should find out, and that if he was going to share it on social media then at least make it after the event to save me the worry. He laughed and assured me it would be fine, the instructors knew about his back and it would all be good. It turned out that he'd only agreed to it because Amy and her friend were taking the plunge, and he didn't want to seem cowardly in front of this young woman who he was clearly quite smitten with. He was absolutely terrified but, as ever, he faced his fears and

F*ck the Biscuits

did indeed jump from a plane at a height of approximately 10,000 feet. Wow, never in a million years would I have imagined that this would be possible, but it was.

One of his friends came back to the UK early, leaving Aaron and his other mate Ben to travel alone. They shared a campervan, and spent a lot of time together talking. In many ways, this was the beginning of Aaron's spiritual journey. He inevitably had a lot of questions to find the answers to, and did a great deal of soul searching. He knew he had survived the crash for a reason and that he had a purpose in life, but he just didn't know what that was. This felt like a huge responsibility for him. He reached deep and faced his demons, and read several spiritual books on awareness, consciousness and awakening. He also studied the work of Dr. Joe Dispensa who is a world-renowned authority on the power of the mind-body connection and an expert on neuroscience, epigenetics and quantum physics. Somehow Aaron just knew he was heading in the right direction.

It Never Really Ends

These were strange times in many ways, an emotional rollercoaster of extreme highs and lows, both for Aaron and for me. He confessed to me that he had never felt as lonely as he did at times on that trip, realising that wherever he went and whoever he went with, he would always feel lonely because he had lost himself in all of this. He didn't know who he was any more, this led to him digging deep to find himself.

It was a considerable number of years later that I attended a talk that Aaron gave during which he explained that there was a time when he looked in the mirror and didn't know the person looking back at him. When I heard this, it touched my heart. I knew he was struggling but I didn't realise how much, this left me feeling inadequate. I had let him down. I should have realised and understood, yet it wouldn't have changed anything. This was just another thing I couldn't do for him, or take away from him. Ironically, looking back, exactly the same could be said of me, I knew I was struggling but didn't realise how much.

Aaron and Ben visited Fraser Island in Queensland one day while they were in Australia, an absolutely stunning island. It was here that Aaron said he still felt so lost despite the beauty of the place and it was then that he understood that he couldn't run away from how he felt, he had to face it. He told me that learning to walk was not his greatest challenge, not recognising the person in the mirror was the most frightening. This realisation was a huge part of his spiritual journey.

After three months Aaron returned to the UK. It was obvious that the trip had done him the world of good even though he had a long way to go. He still kept in touch with Amy and one night, after a birthday party, Aaron and I sat with some of his friends at my kitchen table drinking shots in the wee small hours - as one does - when he showed me a picture of her on his phone. He said, "Mum, she's the one, I'm going back for her. I'm going to marry her one day!"

He began raising funds to get back to Australia, a lot of which involved selling stuff on eBay. It became a joke to say, "Don't stand still for long or Aaron will sell you!". It was in October 2010 that he got another visa and returned to Australia to see Amy. He did, indeed, bring her home and it was just before Christmas that year when I first met the woman who was to change our lives.

This was such a romantic story. I was so proud and so happy, and would constantly talk about it at work and amongst friends. Aaron was still suffering from ongoing health issues, mainly involving bowel, bladder and sexual function. It also transpired that it was extremely doubtful he would ever be able to have children. This pained me considerably, it all felt so unfair. This affected us all as a family, and as Aaron is my only child it meant I would never be blessed with grandchildren. I tried not to believe this would be the case, despite being afraid of getting my hopes up, I repeatedly reminded myself that these were the same medical experts who said Aaron would never walk again.

I worked hard to keep the faith, and prayed. After all, my prayers had been answered before. Aaron asked for my advice, he wanted to know if he should tell Amy about his issues at this stage. I told him that she had a right to know, and that if she were my daughter, I would want her to know. I also said that if she was the woman he thought she was then she would understand. She was and she did.

I've mentioned that there's never a dull moment when Aaron is involved. One day, out of the blue, he told us that he was going to take part in the London to Paris cycle ride. I was so excited, despite some highs and lows, life was good and this was such a positive and fun thing to do. It would be an enormous challenge though, it involves four days in the saddle covering 310 miles from capital to capital. Aaron was up for it, he bought himself a bike and began a tough and strict training regime.

This time he was to raise money for Sense, a charity for children with complex disabilities, and I began a huge campaign for his sponsorship. Once again, the media got involved and there were several articles published. Just as you would expect 'Man who was told he would never walk again now to ride the London to Paris cycle challenge'... that kind of thing. My customers at work were super generous and showed a great deal of interest in his venture. I felt incredibly proud of my son, as I always do. Would he ever cease to amaze me?

It Never Really Ends

I can categorically say that the answer to this question is most definitely No!

This was a huge event and so a group of us including Mark, Amy, Ant and Sam decided we would go to Paris to see Aaron cross the finishing line. It was a fine day in July 2015, Steve took Aaron to London for the start of the challenge while the rest of us took the Eurostar to Paris. It was so exciting and a real adventure. I'll never forget the look on his face when he came through the finish line, he was completely elated. What an incredible achievement. We had made a banner saying 'Congratulations Aaron' which we held high as he passed us. The atmosphere was electric as we watched him, along with his team mates, being presented with his medal.

It was at dinner that night in a beautiful Parisian restaurant that Aaron told us just how gruelling the journey had been. There were times when he nearly gave up, but he didn't. There's a lesson there for all of us. I was astounded when he told the story of how they came down the home stretch around the Arc de Triomphe then down the Champs-Élysées. The

F*ck the Biscuits

following day was the Tour de France which was to take the same route so there were lots of barriers in place and a lot of tourists gathering in the city. Aaron laughed when he said there were tourists taking photos of them and cheering them on as they whizzed past, probably mistaking them for the Tour de France, and he said it felt just like the visualisation technique he had used on the bike in the gym at Stoke Mandeville, he got to relive that moment for real. How extraordinary this was and it blew my mind. They were much deserved happy times for us all.

A year later came one of the most memorable and joyous days, Aaron and Amy were married. The wedding was truly stunning and extremely emotional. I was so happy, we'd come such a long way. Amy really was the epitome of a beautiful bride and Aaron looked very much the handsome groom. There was so much love and laughter, a time for family and for celebration. The day was perfect. Life was good.

Life got even better... in April 2018 I received more miraculous news. Amy was pregnant. I remember so clearly the two of them telling me and how I held Amy tight and sobbed, another prayer had been answered. It was more than I had dared to hope for. I was elated, happy for them and for myself. I don't know how it became possible, but suffice to say sometimes all it takes is the love of a good woman. On the 3rd November 2018, my darling granddaughter, Ava Rose Timms, was born. She is beautiful and my love for her is limitless. I have always had a close bond with her. From the time she was a baby, I looked after her a couple of days a week while Amy worked. We created some beautiful memories and had fun together, she was my partner in crime. Although we had lots of fun days out, my favourite memories involve cuddling up on the sofa watching a movie and of her having a sleepover at Nanny's house, she loved to stay and was always as good as gold, an absolute pleasure. With Ava, my life felt complete.

Two years later I was to receive news that I really didn't see coming and it rocked my world. Aaron and Amy broke the news that they would be moving out to Bali to enrol Ava into the Green School located there when she was old enough. Just as my heart was

F*ck the Biscuits

healing from the trauma we had been through over the years, it was broken again. I completely understood their reasons and wholly supported their decision but that doesn't mean it wasn't incredibly painful for me. My heart felt as if it had been ripped in two, and I went through what I can best describe as a mourning process. Mourning both the life I was living then and was about to lose, and the life I had imagined to be my future, the times I would spend with my family as my granddaughter was growing up. I had envisaged taking her to all sorts of different places and sharing not only experiences with her as she grew but also my wisdom and compassion. This life I had foreseen was not to be.

On top of this, sadly my marriage to Mark had not been a happy one for a number of years and in October 2021 I made the difficult decision to end the marriage. It was not until after my relationship ended that it became apparent to me that Aaron and Amy would be happy for me to move to Bali with them. Until then the thought of moving to Bali had never occurred to me. I had nothing to lose and everything to gain, including

It Never Really Ends

being a part of Ava's new life. And so another life-changing adventure began.

It was with great excitement and anticipation that, in May 2022, I flew to Bali to start a new life with Aaron, Amy and my beautiful granddaughter Ava. It was tough leaving the people I love behind, but they were so happy for me, and I knew that I had to do this. It was simple, the only thing I would regret was not going and that remains true to this day.

Life had, without a doubt, moved on from that fateful night. But a spinal cord injury never really leaves you, and it never really ends. On the face of it all is well, Aaron has full mobility and leads an active and extremely good life but it's the little things that go on behind closed doors, the things that people don't see or realise, these act as a constant reminder. Aaron has medical issues to deal with pretty much on a daily basis, I once asked him how he felt about that and his response was that he worried about it less than I did, he just got on with it. He was probably right, the feeling of being powerless to help or take it all away will perhaps never leave me.

F*ck the Biscuits

There are times when Aaron suffers chronic back ache, he does after all have metal rods embedded in his spine, and I sometimes wonder if he will always have his demons buried deep, the accident has left its mark on us all. When we were in Bali, Aaron was so excited to surf and had been looking forward to it for a long time. He had a weekend of surfing lessons with a small group booked and off he went with a spring in his step. When he returned, he was happy but it was clear that something was not right. Because of the weakness he will always have in one of his legs, he was not able to surf properly, one of his legs was just too weak.

I felt totally gutted for him and it bothered me much more than I let on. I was angry, I just wanted things to be normal and I hated how unjust it all feels at times. Now if anyone at this point is thinking, "Well, boo hoo!", I get it, totally get it. In the grand scheme of things whether he can surf or not doesn't entirely matter and I understand that there are thousands with spinal cord injury who would love to have that problem, so if I offend then I apologise. I'm simply telling it how it is for me and mine.

It Never Really Ends

We were building a new life in Bali. I was excited and happy, a little apprehensive and also very sad, having left behind the rest of my family and my incredible friends who had been there for me throughout this entire ordeal. We had shared extreme highs and lows and everything in between. I love my friends dearly and moving so far away from them filled me with heartache. Little did I know then that I was about to need them more than ever over the coming months.

CHAPTER ELEVEN

And So the Journey Began

The journey to recovery, to spiritual awareness, to growth, to wisdom and to happiness. "We are spiritual awareness having this human experience." It is with this understanding and perspective that I now lead my life, even though it has taken some extremely difficult times to awaken to my truth.

I think it would be fair to say it is highly unlikely that anyone would have this kind of experience without it leaving a lasting impact. Despite the trauma we went through, or maybe because of it, I am pleased and proud to say that the long-term effect has been to come to a place of spiritual awareness, of wisdom and ultimately of happiness both for Aaron and me. It is my privilege to share some of my lessons with you.

F*ck the Biscuits

One day, the mountain that is in front of you will be so far behind you, it will barely be visible in the distance. But the person you become in learning to get over it? That will stay with you forever. And that is the point of the mountain.

Brianna Wiest

My spiritual journey began after the accident and I'm not sure it will ever end, spiritual growth is a continuous journey. "We are spiritual awareness having this human experience." Such a simple yet profound statement that has transformed the way I approach life and has taken me all of my adult life to understand.

I have always been spiritually aware, even as a child, but I failed to live my life accordingly. I got caught in the trap of life, unable or unwilling to tap into something higher. But now that I live my life being true to myself, I am in a much better place.

Unbeknown to me at the time, my initiation on the spiritual path began with Aaron's accident. I turned to

And So the Journey Began

prayer in my desperation, and my prayers were answered. The spiritual awakening process is complex, multi-layered, and different for everyone. It is often caused by major life traumas and the months, no years, that followed the accident most certainly had their fair share of trauma. Ultimately, anything that encourages or forces you to "look at your life from a more spiritual perspective" can set you on a path toward awakening. Aaron realised that he had been spared his life for a reason, and embarked on a journey of discovery, of self-discovery and of spiritual enlightenment. This encouraged me to follow my path to something much bigger than me, for which I am grateful.

When my prayers, and those of others, were heard, I was fully aware of it. Many would simply dismiss this and I do smile to myself when sceptics say it's all nonsense, they want proof. Okay, all medical specialists were of the professional opinion that Aaron would never walk again. I prayed every night for him to walk, as did many others including prayer groups. Aaron walked again. I ask how much more proof is

F*ck the Biscuits

needed? "I'll believe it when I see it," say the critics, "You'll see it when you believe it," say others. Aaron once described the experience of his accident as the 'dark night of the soul' and it often takes one to reach this depth of despair to embark on a journey of enlightening. I believe this to have been the case for us both.

I had the curiosity of a child, willing to listen and learn. I took my inspiration from many including Eckhart Tolle, Wayne Dyer, Mooji, and Burgs to name but a few. After reading Eckhart Tolle's 'The Power of Now', I understood the importance and significance of being 'present', we don't lead our lives in the past and the future doesn't actually exist so to miss the present moment is to miss life itself, it's the only thing that there truly is. When you focus on the moment of Now then everything is okay, our fears and worries always focus on either the past or the future.

One of the most valuable lessons I learned from Eckhart Tolle was the ability to be a witness to my thoughts. To be the observer, not the thinker. Observing the constant chatter in our minds is a powerful tool to understand and know that we are not our thoughts. Returning to a mindful state whereby you are experiencing only the present moment is like a power nap for the mind. Eckhart's profound, yet simple, teachings have helped me to experience a state of inner peace. His work focuses on the awakened state of consciousness which transcends ego. He sees this awakening as the essential next step in human evolution.

I learned to understand the concept of the ego. It is our self-image, not our true self. We create an identity, often multiple identities, based on our experiences. For example, being starved of love as a child can cause us to create an identity of someone who lacks self-worth. Our true self can never lack self-worth. What we do for a living, where we live, our name, our likes and dislikes - all of these are shaped by our life experiences and are not a representation of who we really are, a spiritual being.

The ego represents the mind and the body, to go beyond that we need to have a level of self-awareness. I have found it hugely rewarding to identify an ego that no longer serves me and let it go. A good example of this is that I have always been a 'chameleon friend', able to adapt to fit my environment. This comes from an ego which told me to blend in to be accepted based on childhood experience. It was while I sat next to a pool in Bali that I had the realisation not only that I do this – become a chameleon - but that it is not necessary. I thought about a bowl of succulent, sweet and beautiful strawberries, no matter how good they are, not everyone will like them. Would you change the strawberries? Of course not, you would simply accept that some people won't like them and that's okay. I saw myself as that bowl of fruit, with no need to change, I am good enough as I am and if some don't like me then that's okay.

This realisation allowed me to release the ego which no longer served me. Self-doubt and fear of judgement are the work of the ego, and the little voice in our heads that tells us all sorts of lies such as 'I'm not good enough', 'What if...?', 'I can't do that'. Whenever those thoughts pass through, I refer to the voice as Jiminy Cricket, sitting on my shoulder telling me a pack of lies, and I literally brush him away telling him I am not interested in his false opinion. That's what I mean by a level of awareness, being mindful of our thoughts.

I will probably always have a battle with fear of judgement and self-doubt, but now I have the weapon to win the fight. I overcame a huge fear of judgement by writing this book. Now I simply understand and accept that, just like the strawberries, not everyone will like it, but some will. It took a conversation one night with some wonderful people who saw me for who I truly am, who understood what I have to offer by sharing my story, for me to put my fears and doubts behind me and speak my truth. I will be forever grateful to Dora and Rob, whom I met in Bali, and the part that they unwittingly played in the creation of this book.

WHO IS THIS

(A poem written to describe the Ego)

I came out alone on my way to my tryst
But who is this that follows me in the silent dark?

F*ck the Biscuits

I move aside to avoid his presence but I escape him not

He makes the dust rise from the earth with his swagger

He adds his loud voice to every word that I utter

He's my own little self My Lord

He knows no shame

But I am ashamed to come to your door in his company

Rabindranath Tagore

And So the Journey Began

I have been truly blessed with some incredible friends but not everyone 'gets' me and it was several years ago that I felt I needed someone else to share my spiritual path. So I began an attempt to manifest this person, who I imagined to be female with an open and enlightening mind. Some weeks later, as I walked through the meadows near me with my dog, I noticed a woman walking towards me with her two dogs. I had never seen her before but our pups were taking an interest in each other so we stopped to chat, and within minutes we were having a really deep and meaningful conversation about life and the Universe.

Faye was a yoga tutor with her own studio very close to my home. This was the start of my yoga and spiritual practice which served me extremely well. It was through yoga, which is deeply rooted in spirituality, and with Faye's guidance that I understood and experienced the benefit of meditation. In addition, yoga not only improved my physical strength and flexibility, but also enhanced my emotions, mentality and concentration. This ancient science goes far beyond the mere physical aspects, by way of deepening the connection between mind, body and most important of all, the spirit. The years spent with Faye as my mentor and tutor were a blessing, and played a huge part in taking me to where I am today.

Learning to trust and recognise my instinct now plays a big part in my life. When you know, you know. The voice in your head that instinctively knows, I see it as guidance from the Universe, from my spiritual team-mates. It is my belief that our spirit team was assigned to us before we entered into our physical body and is here to guide, comfort, protect and reassure our soul on its earthly journey. The more we invite their guidance in, the stronger the role they will play in our lives. They have a deep understanding of the soul lessons that we need to learn in this lifetime and can offer guidance, support and clarity and will always point us to the right answer.

There are times when I hear something said which I know to be an absolute truth, a definite way forward, a correction action or intent. I know this to be so because I experience what I now call my 'truth shivers', shivers that run uncontrollably up my spine at which point I recognise that what I am hearing is authentic, a certainty. But I don't need to feel my 'truth shivers' to follow my instinct, the knowing feeling that we have. It was a voice in Aaron's head on the night of the accident that told him to get in the back of the car, it was the thing that not only saved his life but took him on the path he treads today. Trust the Universe, trust what is.

Another lesson I have learned is to have an 'attitude of gratitude', being thankful has a huge effect on our state of mind. When we are grateful for what we have, for being loved and cared for, when we appreciate the beauty of nature or all the good and positive in our lives, it puts us in a frame of mind whereby we feel fulfilled instead of feeling in a state of lack and inadequacy. Showing this same gratitude when things don't go so well or how we had planned and hoped has an even greater impact. When we experience difficult times or situations, there is always something to be grateful for, whether it is the lesson to be learned from the experience, or maybe the detour that this situation offers protecting us from an otherwise unknown and

F*ck the Biscuits

likely unpleasant outcome. Again, this automatically puts us in a different mindset, taking the power away from that negativity.

The next time you find yourself in a traffic jam, instead of stressing about a situation that you are powerless to change, be grateful for the opportunity to sit and peacefully listen to the radio, or to be afforded the time in your busy life to be able to just sit and 'be' for a short while. You get the picture. It is hugely liberating when you break free from what easily becomes the stress and strain of life. All of this is best summed up by this simple and powerful quote: *'It is not joy that makes us grateful, it is gratitude that makes us joyful.'*

I regularly see and hear people getting wound up and agitated about situations that they are unable to change or which, frankly, are not their concern. On that note, it is also important to be aware of thoughts of envy and jealousy. Be happy for others' good fortune, a state of envy sends the message to our psyche that we are in a state of lack. Be aware of all the negative thoughts too, they can infect our lives and often go unnoticed – when we're thinking 'on

And So the Journey Began

autoplay'. Buddha said *'What you think you become. What you feel you attract. What you imagine you create.'* This is why an awareness of my thoughts is so important to me in my everyday life.

It takes time and effort to understand our truth, to benefit from teachings and advice. I had to put the work in. I studied the books, listened to podcasts, meditated, took notice and made the effort to understand and take action, whether mentally or physically. I dug deep and took the lessons that resonated with me. It's been an interesting, fulfilling and sometimes difficult journey but it has been incredibly worthwhile. Don't get me wrong, I experience times of stress and worry, but I have the tools to change my mindset and have an inner sense of peace. I love this poem by Marianne Williamson, it talks about our relationship with our ego and the liberation of letting that go to truly shine.

F*ck the Biscuits

OUR GREATEST FEAR

It is our light not our darkness that most frightens us
Our deepest fear is not that we are inadequate
Our deepest fear is that we are powerful beyond measure.
It is our light not our darkness that most frightens us
We ask ourselves 'Who am I to be brilliant, gorgeous, talented and fabulous?
Actually, who are you not to be?
You are a child of God.
Your playing small does not serve the world.
There's nothing enlightened about shrinking so that other people
won't feel insecure around you.
We were born to make manifest the glory of God that is within us.
It's not just in some of us; it's in everyone.
And as we let our own light shine,
we unconsciously give other people permission to do the same.

And So the Journey Began

As we are liberated from our own fear, our presence automatically liberates others.

Marianne Williamson

In The Four Agreements, a book I studied and took life-changing lessons from, author Don Miguel Ruiz reveals the source of self-limiting beliefs that rob us of joy and create needless suffering. Based on ancient Toltec wisdom, The Four Agreements offers a powerful code of conduct that can transform our lives to a new experience of freedom, true happiness, and love. Not much is known about the ancient Toltecs of central Mexico. They were gone from their cities many years before the Aztecs arrived to build the centre of their culture at what is now Mexico City. The Aztecs used the word 'Toltec' to describe the lost culture and pyramids they discovered in the lands north of them. No one knows why the Toltec culture disappeared sometime in the 12th century. Although these ancient cultures and societies came and went, the deep spiritual understandings that they had passed down through the generations survived. Their powerful truths were given from teacher to student, from master to apprentice. These are the basic principles of The Four Agreements:

BE IMPECCABLE WITH YOUR WORD

Speak with Integrity.

Say only what you mean.

Avoid using the Word to speak against yourself or to gossip.

Use the power of your Word in the direction of truth and love.

DON'T TAKE ANYTHING PERSONALLY

Nothing others do is because of you.

What others say and do is a projection of their own reality, their own dream.

When you are immune to the opinion and action of others,

you won't be the victim of needless suffering.

And So the Journey Began

DON'T MAKE ASSUMPTIONS

Find the courage to ask questions and to express what you really want.

Communicate with others as clearly as you can to avoid

misunderstandings, sadness and drama.

With just this one agreement, you can completely transform your life.

ALWAYS DO YOUR BEST

Your best is going to change from moment to moment;

it will be different when you are healthy as opposed to sick.

Under any circumstance, simply do your best,

and you will avoid self-judgement, self-abuse and regret.

It was a relatively short period of time after we all moved to Bali that I began to recognise it was not for me. I missed my walks in the woodlands and the tranquillity of the English countryside. The traffic in Canggu felt like an assault on my senses, it was crazy. My energy was not in tune with my surroundings. I am a sociable creature but found it difficult to make friends, everyone seemed so much younger than me. It was clear to me that it would be a real challenge to make a life for myself there with nowhere to go to meet people of my own age, and unable to work because of visa restrictions. I had expected a fairly large ex-pat community but, certainly where we were living, this was not the case. I was living with my family who love me dearly, and I them, yet I felt intensely lonely at times. My heart ached for the people I had left behind and the familiarity of what I will always consider 'home'. Aaron and Amy were starting a new and exciting adventure and I didn't want to spoil it for them so I kept a lot of how I felt to myself.

I also knew that it was time to face my demons, I had nowhere to run and nowhere to hide. Many nights were spent crying myself to sleep, to the point where sometimes my emotions would seem so overwhelming that they would scare me. It was my time to try and make sense of everything and to heal from my marriage. To let go and move forward. Aaron could sense that something was wrong, we did talk and both him and Amy did everything they could to support me, but I couldn't settle.

It started to dawn on me that the reason I had gone to Bali was not to start a new chapter but in fact to end an old one. I allowed the grief for my marriage to spill over, and the negative energy I had unwittingly stored slowly filtered away, gradually releasing and letting go. My heart had been closed for a long time, this was my opportunity to allow it to open up again and to really find myself. Often we need to step outside our comfort zone to do this, to strip away the layers, and I certainly did that! There were times when it got to a point where I was having anxiety attacks, something I have never experienced before, I felt uneasy even just leaving my room some days. All of this was part of my journey... to find my true self, to let go and to become a better person with a much greater level of empathy. Now I understood how it felt to be afraid and to battle emotions that are overwhelming. By allowing the

F*ck the Biscuits

emotions, negative energy and fear to come to the surface I was able to strip away the layers and find my real self. This is so true...

> *Finding yourself is not how it works.*
> *You're not a ten dollar note in last winter's coat pocket.*
> *You are also not lost.*
> *Your true self is right there,*
> *Buried under cultural conditioning, other people's opinions,*
> *and inaccurate conclusions you drew as a kid that became your beliefs about who you are.*
> *Finding yourself is actually returning to yourself.*
> *An unlearning, an excavation,*
> *A remembering of who you were before the world got its hands on you.*
>
> **Emily McDowell**

And So the Journey Began

I didn't have to go through this all alone though. Despite the distance, my friends back home were there for me yet again. They poured messages of love and support just when I needed it the most, I felt them there with me. Jan took a video call from me at 3 o'clock in the morning. I was sobbing and wanted to see her kind face and hold her so tight. I must have looked such a mess. We both cried, she said all the right things and eventually eased my pain. She always eases my pain. Jan wasn't the only one, Sue was on the receiving end of a similar call too. She also cried with me. I reached out and took strength from every single one of my incredible friends, each played a part in their own way for which I am forever grateful.

I certainly made the most of my time in Bali and enjoyed lots of memorable experiences with my family. We spent a weekend with friends on the north of the island and whilst we were there, we visited an absolutely beautiful Buddhist Temple where I had an incredible experience. Despite enjoying my weekend in beautiful surroundings with friends who were very good company, welcoming hosts and wise souls, I was

F*ck the Biscuits

struggling this particular day and was feeling tearful, lost and uncertain about my future. I knew deep down that Bali and this new life were not for me but was still not sure which way my life should be heading. At times I felt like a lost and lonely child.

When we got to the temple, I wandered off alone, this was my kind of place and I wanted to explore on my own. Amy totally understood my need for solitude and left me to it. I walked around the grounds looking for a suitable place to sit quietly and meditate, to try to clear my head. There were plenty of opportunities but nothing felt quite right, until I found myself inside the temple in the shrine room. There were a couple of other people there in quiet meditation so I gently and respectfully sat down, feeling peaceful and at home with a sense of belonging.

I closed my eyes for a while and when I opened them what I saw before me was extraordinary, there was a path in front of me. It didn't appear as my imagination, it looked completely real. A simple yet clear path ahead of me, not necessarily straight but the message was obvious, the path in front of me was clear in two ways. There were no obstacles along the way, and the vision itself was so clear. I had been given a sign. Take a look at your surroundings right now, what I saw before me was just as real and defined. I knew then that all I had to do was follow my heart and whatever I did, wherever I found myself, it would be right for me. My path ahead was clear. I have never experienced anything quite so remarkable and it has stayed with me ever since. After a while the vision faded and I made my way back out into the gardens to look for the others. I saw Amy and it was as if she knew. She smiled kindly at me then reached out to hug me, I felt extremely emotional yet at peace for the first time in a long while as we held each other tightly with love in our hearts.

Sitting in the garden at our villa one afternoon, Aaron told me that I was the reason he believed in himself, that I had brought him up to do just that for which he will be forever grateful, and that now it was time for me to believe in myself. The love between us was palpable. I am indebted to Aaron and all that he has given me, for the opportunity, for the love, for being

F*ck the Biscuits

the best son I could possibly wish for. I was truly blessed the day he was born. Without him I wouldn't be the person I am today. It was this conversation that led me to understand that it was time for both of us to lead our own lives. I am proud of my son, I always have been and always will be, and I am proud of what I have achieved as a mother. I've made lots of mistakes along the way but somehow I got it right in the end. I had taken Aaron to this point, now it was time for me to lead my own life. One of my favourite books is The Prophet by Khalil Gibran, a writer and philosopher, who has this to say about children...

And a woman who held a babe against her bosom said Speak to us of Children.

And he said:

Your children are not your children.

They are the sons and daughters of Life's longing for itself.

They come through you but not from you,

And though they are with you yet they belong not to you.

And So the Journey Began

You may give them your love but not your thoughts.
For they have their own thoughts.
You may house their bodies but not their souls,
For their souls dwell in the house of tomorrow, which you cannot visit, not even in your dreams.
You may strive to be like them, but seek not to make them like you.
For life goes not backward nor tarries with yesterday.
You are the bows from which your children as living arrows are sent forth.
The archer sees the mark upon the path of the infinite, and He bends you with His might that His arrows may go swift and far.
Let your bending in the archer's hand be for gladness;
For even as He loves the arrow that flies, so He loves also the bow that is stable.

Khalil Gibran

I had to move on, to leave my family to lead their own lives whilst I did the same. So it was that in August

F*ck the Biscuits

2022 I broke the news to Aaron and Amy that I would be going back to the UK the following month. We all cried and hugged each other, but they completely understood and knew it was coming. I promised them that if they ever needed me, I would be there in a heartbeat, I meant it then and always will. Seeing Aaron's reaction and the tears I had caused filled me with that familiar feeling of guilt. I felt like I had let him down, but of course this wasn't true, it was simply my narrative. He was just hurting at the thought of not having me directly in his life anymore, and I felt the same. He also had concerns that I was making the wrong decision, but I knew in my heart it was the right one.

It had been a very difficult decision to make but not one that I had faced entirely alone. I still had an amazing network of friends back in the UK who held my hand while I made my choice. It was advice from a dear lifelong friend, Loraine, that made things clearer in my head. Loraine seems to understand and know me better than I do at times. She told me that it was time to be true to myself, that it was okay to just be me.

And So the Journey Began

She made me see that coming home was the right thing to do. Her friendship knows no bounds and when I went back to the UK she gave me a home, somewhere to stay in peace and tranquillity while I got on my feet. I hope she knows how indebted I am to her for her love, her wisdom and her generosity.

Looking back, I can see that I played a huge part in helping my family to settle into their new life in Bali. I had shared this experience with Ava and seen her settled at her new school, witnessing for myself just how happy she is, how she loves her school and is meeting new friends. Living her best life. To visit her school on several occasions and be a part of this was an absolute honour for which I am eternally thankful.

It was sad to leave my family behind and heartbreaking to leave Ava. Saying goodbye to her was one of the hardest things I have done. On the day I left, I waved her off to school in the morning and she understood that I would not be there when she returned at the end of the day. As she was about to get in the car with the other children she looked back, ran up to me and hugged me tightly. In that moment she took a piece of my heart which will always belong to her no matter where life takes her. I had to be a brave nanny and waved her goodbye before sobbing uncontrollably once I was out of her sight.

Later that morning I got into a taxi with my cases, having said a tearful and emotional goodbye to Aaron and Amy. It was not what I expected, but I really did feel okay. I was ready to do this and looking forward to moving on with my own life. In honesty, I was feeling quite adventurous, travelling such a long way on my own and starting a new chapter for which I had no definite plans. However, that all changed on the plane.

As we gathered speed on the runway, it felt like my emotions were in sync with the aircraft. The engines roared and the pressure built up and it was as if something inside me was preparing to lift as well. Suddenly it came, an overwhelming heartbreak. As the plane left the ground and I left Bali behind, my heart broke in two, all I could see in my mind was Ava and I wanted to tell her how sorry I was for leaving her and that I love her more than she could ever know.

Suffice to say I was grateful when the seatbelt light went off so I could go to the toilets and clean up my face which was in a mess from the crying that I simply couldn't hold back despite being amongst all the other passengers. As everyone, myself included, settled down for the long journey my pain began to dissipate and I felt good again knowing that I was following my path and grateful that I had learned so much and experienced so much. My energy was cleansed, my experience had been spiritually awakening and the closure of a chapter. I was ready for the new one to begin. In every respect my time in Bali had been an absolute gift.

Within a matter of weeks after arriving back in the UK I had somewhere to live, an income and a car. It was all just so easy, my return was clearly meant to be. There were no obstacles in my way, the path ahead was clear. Just like I had seen in the temple several months before. It slowly dawned on me that this was the first time in my adult life that I had no-one to look after or be responsible for other than myself. It is a very unfamiliar yet liberating feeling.

F*ck the Biscuits

I am pleasantly surprised at how quickly I have adjusted to living so far apart from Aaron, Amy and Ava. Of course we miss each other but we are all where we are supposed to be and life is good for us all. We do what we can to make it work, and it does. I love to see the photographs of them in which you can clearly see that they are truly happy. Their happiness is my happiness. We send each other videos and they record any significant moments. A good example was opening the Christmas parcel I sent them. I could see the excitement in their faces and hear it in their voices, it enabled me to share the moment with them. I regularly speak to Ava on video call which is always a joy and reassures me that she hasn't forgotten me, an unnecessary and unfounded concern of mine to begin with. I soon understood that the foundation we have built and the love we have can never be shaken by the miles between us. Inevitably there are times when I miss them terribly, especially Ava, and although it saddens me I understand that it is perfectly natural and to be expected.

And So the Journey Began

The icing on the cake is that I now have a new man in my life, someone who makes me happy. I feel safe, supported, respected, loved and understood. A reflection of the love I have for myself. We spent our first Christmas together in 2022 which was, ironically, the first Christmas without my family. I spoke to Aaron, Amy and Ava on Christmas morning and it was a joy to see my little family so happy and so excited to talk to me.

Reflecting on the new year ahead I thought about how Aaron and his family are living their dream in Bali, and the joy that it brings not only them but me too. Aaron has found the happiness he truly deserves at long last, and I believe I have as well. I start the new year knowing that my man will always care for me and have my back, whatever this year brings it will be better with him by my side. I am extremely grateful for the love I share with my friends who have been with me, and supported me, throughout this entire journey and will remain forever in my heart.

CHAPTER TWELVE

And Finally

This is my story and my account of events from a mother's perspective. For some involved in the journey there will be elements which may not ring true for them, and for some it will be an eye opener. This is the story of a mother's love, told from the heart with honesty and integrity.

If you, or anyone you love, has been affected by Spinal Cord Injury or any other life-changing condition, my heart and love goes out to you. If I were to offer just one piece of advice, it would be that the prognosis doesn't necessarily have to become a self-fulfilling prophecy. To my dying day I will always believe that if Aaron knew the truth of what had been said in the early days, he would have lost his hope and belief, and would not have learned to walk again. I get that giving false hope is cruel, but no-one has the right to take

F*ck the Biscuits

away hope - it's yours to keep and do with what you will.

I also completely understand that every injury is different, every person and situation is different. But the one thing we have in common are the worries, frustration, anger, sadness, fear and overwhelmingly - particularly as a parent - a sense of deep-rooted helplessness and powerlessness. The anguish occupies the mind every minute of every day, it's exhausting and relentless. To see your child broken and know that there is nothing you can do to fix them is pain beyond words. Take heart, don't lose hope for the future, whatever the extent of the injury, whatever the outcome - love will find a way.

My wish is that you will be able to take something from my story, that maybe a part of this book landed for you and resonated with you. Take from it what you need.

Every experience, no matter how bad it seems, holds within it a blessing of some kind. The goal is to find it.

Buddha

And Finally

Aaron now works as a professional trainer and coach. He is the founder of Conscious Success and the Superconscious Training Academy, his focus is to help others live a life of purpose and meaning. After the accident, he dedicated his life to understanding human potential and how to unlock the potential that lies dormant in everyone. Now he is focused on helping people restore their superconscious abilities and create a life of total freedom. Financial, physical, mental, emotional and spiritual freedom. He wrote his first book, Belief Bound Mind, in 2018 and his second book, Everything Starts With You, was published in 2022. Both of these books are available on Amazon.

One of Aaron's clients wrote a review in which he stated, "I want to express my gratitude towards Aaron Timms. If you're looking for a way to discover the real you and unlock parts of you that you didn't even know existed then I really do advise you to speak to him. He is a magnificent person and is brilliant at what he does." In response, Aaron said, "Ever since that day when I walked out of hospital after being told I would never walk again I have been obsessed with human potential. Now I get the honour and privilege of unlocking the potential within other people. Thank you to anybody who has ever placed their trust in me and allowed me to work with them." For further details of Aaron's work and the programmes he delivers, you can visit his website www.aarontimmsofficial.com.

I leave you with this poem by Jeff Foster. Please know that inside you are that warrior.

HOW I BECAME A WARRIOR

Once, I ran from Fear

so fear controlled me.

Until I learned to hold fear like a newborn.

Listen to it, but not give in.

Honour it, but not worship it.

Fear could not stop me anymore.

I walked with courage into the storm.

I still have fear,

but it does not have me.

And Finally

Once, I was Ashamed of who I was.
I invited shame into my heart.
I let it burn.
It told me 'I am only trying to protect your vulnerability'.
I thanked shame dearly,
and stepped into life anyway,
unashamed, with shame as a lover.

Once, I had great Sadness buried deep inside.
I invited it to come out and play.
I wept oceans. My tear ducts ran dry.
And I found joy right there.
Right at the core of my sorrow.
It was heartbreak that taught me how to love.

Once, I had Anxiety.
A mind that wouldn't stop.
Thoughts that wouldn't be silent.
So I stopped trying to silence them.

F*ck the Biscuits

And I dropped out of the mind, and into the Earth.
Into the mud.
Where I was held strong like a tree,
unshakable, safe.

Once, Anger burned in the depths.
I called anger into the light of myself.
I felt its shocking power.
I let my heart pound and my blood boil.
Listened to it, finally.
And it screamed 'Respect yourself fiercely now!'
'Speak your truth with passion!'
'Walk your path with courage!'
'Let no one speak for you!'
Anger became an honest friend.
A truthful guide.
A beautiful wild child.

Once, Loneliness cut deep.
I tried to distract and numb myself.

And Finally

Ran to people and places and things.
Even pretend I was 'happy'.
But soon I could not run anymore.
And I tumbled into the heart of loneliness.
and I died and was reborn
Into an exquisite solitude and stillness.
That connected me to all things.
So I was not lonely, but alone with All Life.
My heart One with all other hearts.

Once, I ran from Difficult Feelings.
Now, they are my advisors, confidants, friends,
and they have a home in me,
and they all belong and have dignity.
I am sensitive, soft, fragile,
my arms wrapped around all my inner children.
And in my sensitivity, power.
In my fragility, an unshakeable Presence.

In the depths of my wounds,

F*ck the Biscuits

in what I had named 'darkness'.
I found a blazing Light
that guides me now in battle.
I became a warrior when I turned towards myself.
And started listening

Jeff Foster

Thank you for allowing me to share my innermost thoughts, my fears, the rollercoaster ride and the lessons. May you hold on to hope and belief no matter where your own journey has taken you and wherever your path may lead.

The last word goes to Aaron, he once delivered these words at a public event as tears sprung to his eyes and sorrow encompassed his face...

"Every single moment of every single day it felt like these invisible walls of fear were caving in on me,
I felt like there was no way out.

And Finally

I wanted to walk as much as I wanted to breathe.
I had to fight for everything – physio, belief in me.
If I can find light in my darkest hour then you can too.
All it took was hope and belief."

Printed in Great Britain
by Amazon